250

THE ROOT OF THE VINE

THE ROOT OF THE VINE

Essays in Biblical Theology

by

ANTON FRIDRICHSEN

AND OTHER MEMBERS OF UPPSALA UNIVERSITY

INTRODUCTION BY A. G. HEBERT, D.D., S.S.M.

PHILOSOPHICAL LIBRARY
NEW YORK

PUBLISHED 1953
BY PHILOSOPHICAL LIBRARY INC.
15 EAST 40TH STREET, NEW YORK 16, N.Y.

PRINTED IN GREAT BRITAIN FOR PHILOSOPHICAL LIBRARY
BY NEILL AND CO. LTD., EDINBURGH

INTRODUCTION

THIS collection of essays was planned in the first place by Dom Gregory Dix. When he visited Sweden in 1950, he made up his mind that the school of New Testament scholarship which he found there, particularly at Uppsala, deserved to be better known in England. Had he lived, it would have been his part to see this book through the press and to write the Introduction. It falls to me to write it, because of my friendship with him on the one hand, and on the other because of my acquaintance with the Swedish Church which goes back now some twenty-four years.

When after a long interval I visited Sweden again after Easter this year, I began immediately to learn how remarkably Dom Gregory had endeared himself to my own Swedish friends. Those who knew him will not be surprised to hear that when I had dinner one afternoon with a learned Doctor at Uppsala (one who does not happen to be a contributor to this volume), I found that to his little sons Dom Gregory was *farbror munken*, "Uncle Monk"; and that when he had started on his journey home the Doctor had described to the boys the motions of the ship at sea, and the probable effects on their beloved "Uncle".

These essays were worth collecting and publishing; for important work has been done in Sweden recently in the region of Biblical studies, particularly through the influence of Anton Fridrichsen, for some twenty years the New Testament Professor at Uppsala. He has trained up a splendid array of scholars, and I believe all the authors of these essays are his old pupils. The *Acta Seminarii Neotestamentici Upsaliensis* already consist of nineteen books, issued under his editorship, and written for the most part in English or French or German. At the time of writing, Dr Fridrichsen has just retired from the professorship, and it is certain that one or another of his pupils will succeed him.

These essays represent a type of Biblical study very different

v

from that which was common, there as here, a quarter of a century ago. Then, the interest of scholars lay primarily in the documentary analysis of the books, or in archæology, or in the history of Biblical religion. These studies are important, and the newer typological exegesis does not neglect them; but it takes a different view of the Bible as a whole, through its perception that the Bible has a unity of its own, which springs out of a continuous tradition of a living faith. In the Old Testament period Israel had lived as the People of God, united to Him by the Covenant, and had looked forward to the eschatological consummation of His Purpose for mankind in the awaited Day of the Lord; the New Testament writers in their turn saw the work of Jesus as itself the consummation of this Purpose in history, while still looking forward to its final consummation in His Advent. Therefore the imagery which they used to explain the meaning of what Jesus had done was necessarily the imagery of the Old Testament.

We have then a typological exegesis very different in character from the allegorical interpretation which has often and deservedly been criticized as forced and arbitrary; for this exegesis rests first on the history of the events, and then on the "literal sense" of the prophetic and the apostolic writings in which the events are interpreted. The effort of the exegete is to avoid the ever-present danger of reading meanings of his own into the text, and to gain insight and understanding to discern aright the meanings which the Biblical writers put there.

This collection of essays owes very much to the care with which it has been revised, as regards the English phrasing, and prepared for the press by the Rev. H. E. J. Cowdrey, Tutor at St Stephen's House, Oxford.

Kelham, Newark
  October, 1952

A. G. HEBERT, S.S.M.

CONTENTS

I

THE THEOLOGY OF CREATION IN THE OLD AND NEW TESTAMENTS

Gösta Lindeskog

I

I AM ENGAGED in writing a study of the theology of Creation in the New Testament, with due reference to its Old Testament background and to the literature of the period between the Old and the New Testaments. In my contribution to the present volume I should like to anticipate some of my conclusions and to discuss briefly the main aspects of this subject.

Speculations about creation [1] are to be found in all parts of the world. Modern psychologists speak of *artificialism* as a general element in primitive thought.[2] Questions about the Maker of all things occur to primitive people as well as to children.

It is therefore natural to ask what importance the subject of creation has for the study of Biblical theology. It is implicit in the very concept of God that He was a Creator, and the manner in which He created the world is of central importance for the higher religions. Faith in God the Creator is an integral part of the Christian creed and way of worship. But does the Bible really advance beyond conceptions which men borrowed from the stock of ideas common to all ancient religions? Is there a specifically Biblical doctrine of creation?

[1] There is no current term for the doctrine of creation to match such terms as Christology, Eschatology or Soteriology. The term Protology is sometimes used, but it is not everywhere applicable since creation is not always thought of as an initial creation of the world. The lack of a satisfactory name is troublesome, and I propose to use the term Ktisiology.
[2] To the best of my knowledge the term is a coinage of Jean Piaget.

A

II

In this essay we cannot delay to preface our discussion of the Old Testament with an exhaustive exposition of all the ways in which the doctrine of creation can be treated. We must by-pass the elaborate findings of the schools of religious tradition and history, and concentrate our whole attention upon Biblical theology as such. Within the centuries during which the traditions and beliefs recorded in the Old Testament were maturing, they were revised and reshaped by successive generations. Our concern is with the large measure of unity which the theology of the Old Testament manifests in the very latest stages of its literary history.[1]

The final settlement of the text of the Old Testament at about the beginning of the Christian era was due to the development of the dogmatic system of Judaism, which can be traced back to the days of Deutero-Isaiah. It is important that the Old Testament took its final and authorized form just before the life of Jesus Christ. It is often argued that there was a great gap between the Old Testament and Jesus Christ, whereas in point of historical fact the canon of the Old Testament was settled very nearly at the time of His earthly life.

The influence of the idea of creation on earlier Hebrew religion is difficult to trace. The J creation narrative in Genesis, which is very ancient, proves the importance of cosmological speculation at an early date. The traditions behind the Priestly narrative seem also to have been domestic to Israel at a very early time.[2]

G. von Rad suggests that the Yahwist, who represents the

---

[1] For this whole problem, see especially the recent book by Gunnar Östborn, *Cult and Canon: a Study in the Canonization of the Old Testament.* Acta Universitatis Uppsaliensis. 1950.

[2] Cp. the remark of Gerhard von Rad: "Mag seine letzte Ausformung zu der uns hier vorliegenden Gestalt erst in der Exilszeit fallen; seine Wurzeln und Ausgänge liegen gewiss schon im Schoss der ältesten Jahvegemeinde verborgen" (Das erste Buch Mose Kap. i–xii. 3, in *Das Alte Testament Deutsch,* 2, 1949, p. 50).

first great stage in Old Testament historical writing, made his most original contribution to Hebrew tradition when he placed at the beginning of his work the so-called "pre-history" in Genesis ii. 4b–xii. 3. His purpose was to show how sin came into the world and corrupted the creation of God. This is the background against which the election of Abraham must be understood.[1] If von Rad is correct, the position of the J creation story at the beginning of the earliest Old Testament historical narratives bears signal witness to the importance of cosmological thinking in the earlier stages of Hebrew religion.

If the cultic historians are right, the foundation of a kingdom in Israel gave rise to a new cultus in which creation had a central position.[2] Hints of the general Semitic mythology of creation are common in Old Testament poetry. But after the exile, mythological passages lost their original meaning and importance, and survived as mere metaphors, with a more or less spiritualized meaning.[3] The Priestly Creation narrative of Genesis i. 1–ii. 4a is an example of this. The mythology of the story has been drastically expurgated to exclude pre-monotheistic ideas. Surviving expressions which originated in the old creation myth have lost their original meaning.[4]

The Priestly account of the Creation, as it took shape in the last stages of the formation of the Pentateuch, strongly

[1] *Op. cit.*, p. 15 f.

[2] S. Mowinckel (*Psalmenstudien*, II) held that the central theme of the supposed New Year Festival at Jerusalem was the new Creation. Cp. S. H. Hooke: "Old Testament scholars have been rather reluctant to accept Mowinckel's theory that the Processional Psalms imply the existence among the Hebrews of a New Year Festival of the enthronement of Yahweh. But the existence of such a ceremony seems to be extremely probable" (*Myth and Ritual* (1933), p. 13). The same seems to have been the case with the Passover. Cp. G. Östborn, *Cult and Canon*, p. 99: "The fundamental idea of this feast is the thought of a renewal of life, a new creation." Other modern studies of divine kingship and its cultic rôle are Ivan Engnell, *Studies in Divine Kingship in the Ancient Near East* (1943), and Geo. Widengren, *Till det sakrala kungadömets historia i Israel* (in *Horae Söderblomianae I*, Mélanges Johs. Pedersen, fasc. III, 1947), and H. Frankfort, *Kingship and the Gods: a Study of Ancient Near Eastern Religion as the Integration of Society and Nature* (1948).

[3] Cp. Otto Eissfeldt, *Einleitung in das Alte Testament* (1934), p. 225: "Der Werdegang des Pentateuchs bedeutet eine fortwährende Neutralizierung des älteren Bestandes durch das neu hinzutretende Gut."

[4] Cp. S. H. Hooke, *In the Beginning* (1948), p. 35.

insists that the one God was the creator of all things. The Israelites took some time to understand fully the consequences of an exclusively monotheistic faith. But in Deutero-Isaiah there is unquestionably a clear monotheism, and this was crucial for the whole course of later Jewish thought.[1] Equally truly, however, this monotheism was taking shape in Israelite thought long before Deutero-Isaiah. The monolatry or henotheism of the decalogue could scarcely avoid coming to maturity in the clear and exclusive monotheism of the sixth century. The very nature of the God of Moses and the pre-exilic prophets was such that He could not ultimately tolerate other Gods but Himself.[2]

The place occupied by the doctrine of creation in Old Testament religion cannot be understood in isolation from the Yahwism which was central to it, and which distinguishes it sharply from the general run of Near Eastern religions. The religion of the Old Testament is theocentric, and the Old Testament is everywhere concerned with Yahweh's activity. This activity is especially clear in the election and the covenant, the foundations of "a new and good order brought about by Yahweh".[3]

But if the centrality and the nearness of Yahweh invest with their true meaning all other conceptions in the Old Testament, the creation was still a very important element in Hebrew religion. It cannot reasonably be relegated to a subordinate place. G. von Rad is inconsistent with his truer observations when he writes: "Die äussere Stellung der Schöpfungsgeschichte hat oft zu dem Missverständnis geführt, als sei die 'Lehre' von der Schöpfung ein zentraler Gegenstand des alttestamentlichen Glaubens. Das ist aber nicht der Fall. Weder hier, noch bei Deuterojesaja

---

[1] Cp. H. H. Rowley, *The Rediscovery of the Old Testament* (1946), p. 92.

[2] Cp. P. S. Minear, *Eyes of Faith: a Study in the Biblical Point of View* (1946), p. 24: "Monotheism is a corollary of the exclusive claim of Jahweh, rather than a conceptual hypothesis resulting from man's effort to gain a unitary view of his world. It is important, therefore, to distinguish Biblical monotheism from theosophical monism." See also W. F. Albright, *Archæology and the Religion of Israel* (2nd ed., 1946), pp. 116, 119, and *From the Stone Age to Christianity* (2nd ed., 1946), pp. 207, 239, 250.

[3] G. Östborn, *Cult and Canon*, p. 76.

geschieht die Bezeugung der Schöpfung um ihrer selbst willen. Der Schöpfungsglaube ist weder der Standort noch der Zielpunkt der Aussagen in 1 Mos. i und ii. Vielmehr stehen sovohl Jahvist wie Priesterschrift grundsätzlich im Heils- und Erwählungsglauben." [1]

Old Testament religion did not take shape through mythological and metaphysical speculations, but through prophetic encounters with Yahweh. There is little speculation in the Bible. But personal experience of the Holy One was combined with the faith that He is the Creator and Ruler of all, and this fusion of personal and ethical faith in the Holy One and the idea of a Creator-God are what made Hebrew religion so revolutionary in the Near East, and created the possibility of a more universalist type of belief.

For universalism was very far from being originally an integral part of Hebrew religion. The covenant between Yahweh and his people was exclusive and particularist. The national history of Israel—the call of Abraham, the Exodus, the covenant on Sinai, the entry into Canaan and so forth—is the principal interest not only of the historical writers but also of the poets and prophets.

We may here recall the connection of the story of the Exodus with the myth of creation.[2] This can mean one of two things: either the idea of creation is subordinated as the background and pattern of the central event in Israelite history, or the parallel is drawn specifically to emphasize the importance of the Exodus by equating it with the creation of the world. Only thus can the importance of the creation of the chosen people be sufficiently expressed, and I personally prefer the latter alternative.

But even in pre-exilic prophecy, signs of universalism begin to appear,[3] and, in Deutero-Isaiah, universalism and monotheism are both developed to the furthest possible limit. This is no coincidence. Deutero-Isaiah's especial contribution to Old Testament prophecy is to make clear how

---

[1] *Das Alte Testament Deutsch*, 2, p. 34.
[2] See, for instance, Isa. xliii. 16–17, li. 9–10; Ezek. xxix. 3, xxxii; Job xl.
[3] Cp., for example, Gen. xii. 3*b*.

universalism is implicit in monotheism. As a consequence, the theology of creation also comes into its own in a way which is unique among Near Eastern religions. In post-exilic times there exists, beside the traditional national religion, a trend of religious thought in which monotheism, universalism and the theology of creation all gain new significance. But the Jewish idea of the God of the universe is still that traditional belief in a personal, ethical and active God which was typical of Mosaic Yahwism.

Considerable efforts were made to fuse the old and the new in Jewish religion. This is of great importance for the New Testament. The idea that they were the chosen people was indelibly impressed upon the mind of the Jews, and some synthesis between nationalism and universalism had to be attempted. The idea of a chosen people could be understood in more ways than one. The Gentiles might be regarded as simply servants of the chosen people; on the other hand, the chosen people could be thought of as the servant of God through whom the peoples were brought to Him.[1]

This has brought us face to face with the eschatological thinking which originated in exilic and early post-exilic times. We need not discuss here the various factors which stimulated these speculations about the future. We may accept the statement of T. W. Manson: "Eschatology arises from the clash of what is with what ought to be if faith in a God of righteousness is to be maintained."[2] This clash may appear in the guise of national disaster or may have its roots in human sin and the disorder of the world. Especial prominence is given to the idea of creation by eschatological writers. The old world will disappear, but God will create "a new heaven and a new earth" (Isa. lxv. 17, lxvi. 22).

As the idea of election was so characteristic of Israelite religion, it is interesting to see how it was interpreted in a universalist setting which broke through the limits of Israelite history to go back to the creation in an attempt to

[1] Cp. especially H. H. Rowley, *The Biblical Doctrine of Election* (1950).
[2] T. W. Manson, *The Teaching of Jesus: Studies of its Form and Content* (1931), p. 247.

understand God's purpose for mankind. Oscar Cullmann has sought to give a comprehensive account of the term *ecloge* in the following way.[1] When God created the world He made an initial election of man, for man is privileged above all other beings upon earth. His second act of election was when He created His own people. But gradually there was a reduction, as is seen in Isaiah's doctrine of the remnant. Cullmann proceeds to argue that the reduction continues until, as in the beginning, only one man is left—the *'ebed Yahweh* in Deutero-Isaiah and the Son of Man in Daniel. I myself doubt whether these figures are to be understood as simple individuals, as Cullmann suggests, though I grant that the collective interpretation of Isaiah liii is open to objections. I prefer, for the moment, to leave this an open question. The mysterious figure in Daniel vii. 13–14 certainly seems to require a collective interpretation. It is clear, though, that the process of reduction reaches its final stage in 1 Enoch. Here the Son of Man is a real individual. In later Jewish literature, as is well known, the Suffering Servant was interpreted individually; although his experience of suffering was ignored in favour of the conventional Messianism of political and nationalist Judaism.

Turning to the New Testament, we see that Jesus Himself uses Danielic language. T. W. Manson plausibly suggests that Jesus at first understood the Son of Man as meaning the holy remnant.[2] Ultimately, however, He identified Himself with it. He is Himself the Son of Man and the holy remnant. Jesus uses this concept in a double sense. By the Son of Man He means the holy remnant as well as Himself; He is the means by which it will be created. The New Testament writers develop this idea in the image of the Church as the Body of Christ.

We may also notice that the idea of election is combined with that of vicarious suffering; the first writer to do this was Deutero-Isaiah.

---

[1] *Christus und die Zeit. Die urchristliche Zeit und Geschischtsauffassung* (1946), p. 100.
[2] T. W. Manson, *op. cit.*, p. 235.

7

Thus, on the basis of Cullmann, we would make the following parallel:

Old Testament.
  Creation: Adam → The Chosen People → The Remnant.
New Testament.
  The New Creation: The Second Adam → The Church → Mankind.

This parallel is faithful to the Bible, and expresses how its religious thought moved from particularism to universalism. The old prophetic teaching broadened out into this scheme.[1]

The idea of the remnant confirms our view. It originated in horror at the sinfulness of the people. But it belongs by right to the sphere of eschatology, which implies a denial of the present order of things. Ktisiology and eschatology, the beginning and the end, are co-ordinate. Narrow nationalism has been discarded, and the idea of election has gained an enhanced importance and a new meaning.

The process reaches its completion in the New Testament. It is a commonplace nowadays that the Church of the New Testament was anticipated in the Old Testament idea of the chosen people. But what is the relation of the Church to the Kingdom of God? This latter is clearly an eschatological term; it is not yet fully a reality, but it will become so. It is the new order of the future, when evil has been utterly defeated and when God is all in all (1 Cor. xv. 28). As an eschatological fact, the Kingdom of God is the restoration of the world to its created condition before the fall of man.

The Church has also an eschatological significance, but not in the same way as the Kingdom of God. The two concepts are commonly identified, but this is surely a mistake, revealing poverty of thought.[2] The Kingdom of God is, if we may say so, an abstract idea, whereas the Church is a concrete one. The Kingdom of God is the new order, when God rules over his whole creation. The

---

[1] The idea that a single individual plays a decisive rôle in the history of salvation is not, strictly speaking, present in the Old Testament. It was first plainly proposed in such apocalyptic works as 1 Enoch. We can only state the general details of the evolution of this idea. It finds its full maturity in the teaching of Jesus and in his character as Son of Man.

[2] A similar view is to be found in S. H. Hooke, *The Kingdom of God* (1949), p. 69.

8

Church is the gate through which mankind will return to its Source and Creator.

In the Old Testament the people of God was marked off from the remainder of mankind. Even as an historical fact, this separation has religious importance. But it was only a temporary phase. It would be anomalous that just one favoured people should always be the recipient of God's grace. The true Israel is the people of God in the New Testament; everyone can gain citizenship and membership of the body of Christ. There is neither Jew nor Gentile (Gal. iii. 28). There is no separation, but a new unity of all mankind with no restrictive frontiers. In the New Testament the idea of the chosen people remains, but in a new and inclusive sense. Something is achieved which was not possible in the Old Testament: universalism is brought to its complete perfection.

The ground of the fusion between the doctrines of universalism and of creation must be sought in monotheism. God is one and the creator of all things; therefore mankind is a unity.

We must not be content to consider this unity merely from an eschatological point of view. It has another aspect. For this world is itself the creation of God, and because of this, man's present earthly life is also of great importance and significance. The dignity of man follows from his being created in the image of God (Gen. i. 26).[1] And since all men are children of one heavenly Father, sonship is universal, not the exclusive privilege of a favoured few. Everyone is to be regarded as a creature of God, and the necessity of this is the greater when the poor and weak must be defended against the oppression of the rich and powerful.[2]

---

[1] Many other attempts have, of course, been made to explain the words *kidmuṭenu* (i. 26) and *beṣelem 'elohim* (i. 27), but I fully agree with G. von Rad when he says, "Dieses Grundwort *ṣelem* soll nun durch das *demuth* näher erklärt und präzisiert werden, und zwar auch in dem einfachen Sinne, dass dieses Bild dem Urbild entsprechen, dass es ihm ähnlich sein solle" (*Das Alte Testament Deutsch*, 2, p. 45). Cp. Ps. viii., which doubtless expresses the same idea as Gen. i. 26–27. Modern attempts to explain this psalm messianically must be rejected.

[2] Prov. xiv. 31, xxii. 2; Job xxxi. 13 ff., xxxv. 9–10.

This subject only appears in a few places in the Bible, but its importance is very great. It marks the climax of the ethical side of Hebrew religion as embodying the ethical demands implied by faith in the Creator of all. The value and the equality of all men are involved. Man has dignity and worth because he was created in God's image. There is equality among men because there is a single God and a single humanity. And it seems a general rule that what is implicit in the Old Testament becomes explicit in the New.

To summarize, then, we have found three ideas which are fundamental to the Old Testament theology of Creation—monotheism, universalism and the dignity of man. The Priestly narrative of the Creation teaches that there is one God and one humanity, and that man is created in God's image. These three inseparable ideas form the fundamental logic of the Bible. United in the creative act of God, and safeguarded by an insistence that God is one and almighty, they transform generally current ideas of creation and give them an authentic interpretation in prophetic religion. The doctrine of creation lies near the heart of all Biblical thinking.

Further, we have noticed the coalescence of two aspects of Old Testament religion—the national religion of the Covenant, and the prophetic conception of the remnant which becomes progressively narrower until in Enoch it is individualized. This coalescence enabled the writers of the New Testament to speak in the pregnant terms of *Israel cata pneuma* and of the *cainē ctisis* or the new people of God.

Of the two lines which thus coalesced, the national had been limited to the history of the Jewish people. The prophetic line was more universalist and sought its *ultima ratio* in the original act of creation. Eschatology and ktisiology are parallel ideas. The forward anticipation of the old national religion was not really eschatology, but was limited to imminent historical events. The eschatology of later prophecy looked further, to a final end when the old world would end in total catastrophe before the creation of a new heaven and a new earth. This new creation would be the restoration of the original state of creation as it was before the Fall.[1]

The very manner of the synthesis of nationalism and universalism as a transformation of Jewish ideas is the most original contribution of the Old Testament to ktisiology. It was made possible by the experience of the unique character of Yahweh. God has revealed His nature and will to chosen witnesses. Nathan Söderblom [2] has coined the phrase *"the religion of revelation"*, which admirably expresses the uniqueness of Biblical religion. Through the experience of Yahweh's exclusiveness, ethical monotheism was born.

Finally, the Old Testament has two focal points, the creation of the world and the Exodus. The creation concerns all mankind; the Exodus concerns the chosen people. Between these points there was a tension, and movements of attraction and repulsion. But the prophetic movement prepared for their unity, which took place through the New Man, Jesus Christ.

III

The apocalyptic literature of the period between the Old and the New Testaments is of the greatest importance for our subject. The creation narratives of Gen. i.–ii. are the only express treatments of it in Biblical literature. However, this ktisiology gave rise to many speculations, and it was among the functions of apocalyptic literature to elaborate the theology of creation in a comprehensive system of monotheistic ktisiology.[3] The main sources are the Apocalypses of Ezra and of Baruch; I Enoch stands in a class by itself on account of its imagery of the Son of Man.

[1] S. Mowinckel, in his recent work on Messianism (*Han Som Kommer*, 1951), strongly emphasizes the distinction between imminentist futurism and genuine eschatology, which in his opinion was a creation of the apocalyptic writers.

[2] See, for example, *The Living God: Basal Forms of Personal Religion* (1933).

[3] Cp. T. W. Manson, *The Teaching of Jesus* (1931), p. 151: "We cannot expect to understand or value the apocalyptic literature aright unless it is clearly realized that it is a serious attempt to reconcile a faith in omnipotent goodness with the experience of suffering and evil in the world."

For the author of the Apocalypse of Ezra, the fate of the world is a matter of dire consequence. The atmosphere is the same as in the Book of Job; although in Job the problem is the fate of the individual, and here of the whole created order. In both books, however, there is a reasoning with the Creator about the problems of man's existence. Why was he created? Whence does he come? For what purpose was he made? Whence came the sin and evil of this world? How can the Almighty have created a world which is so manifestly disordered? The problems raised by the existence of evil in spite of faith in a good, just and almighty Creator can only be solved if the idea of predestination is invoked. God foresees all things, even the last judgment (2 Esd. vii. 70). Eschatology is thus indispensable to monotheistic ktisiology.

The author of the Ezra Apocalypse takes a very pessimistic view of the present order, but his pessimism is not absolute. There will be a future when God will redeem His creation. This eschatological soteriology is at bottom a doctrine of a new creation, and is therefore a kind of ktisiology.

There is a broad similarity between the Apocalypse of Ezra and the Syriac Apocalypse of Baruch as regards their outlook and their teaching. They are not popular apocalyptic writings, but are elaborately developed and almost philosophical. They stand apart as a new class of literature which we may call "eschatological ktisiology". Ktisiology is very prominent in them; references to the Creator and to creation are especially numerous in the Apocalypse of Baruch. The two books under discussion are capital evidence for the student of later Jewish speculations about the relatedness of the beginning and the end.

This literature forms a useful commentary on the Old Testament, and indicates the teachings about creation which were current in our Lord's day. Jesus must clearly have been familiar with apocalyptic ideas, whatever his own attitude to such forms of speculation. The development of eschatology is the most important feature of post-canonical Jewish literature, and its most fruitful teaching was the idea of the new creation, which was firmly set in a universalist pattern of thought.[1]

IV

How does the theology of creation in the New Testament compare with that in the Old? The brief answer is that the Old Testament teachings are taken over, but given a fresh interpretation arising from the fuller revelation in Christ. The narratives of Creation are accepted, but understood Christologically.[2]

The New Testament is founded on the *kerygma* of the Apostles, that Jesus Christ is the Saviour of the world.[3] The details of early Christian missionary preaching cannot be recovered beyond a certain point. It was addressed to two very different audiences, the Jews and the Hellenistic Gentile world. This distinction can be seen in the Synoptic Gospels; the Gospel of St Matthew is Judaic, and the other two are more Gentile.

Missionary preaching to Jews was expressed in Jewish terms about Jesus as the Messiah of the Jews; so much is clear from the New Testament. How far it bore the marks of Jewish particularism is more debatable. T. W. Manson has assembled evidence for asserting that Jewish eschatology took two different lines.[4] One of them was derived from Ezekiel. Zion will be the centre of the world; the Gentile peoples will at best merely serve Israel and confess that it is the elect race of God. This is universalism of a sort, but it is only a by-product of Jewish particularism. This compromise rests on a nationalism that was certainly foreign to Judaistic Christianity, and cannot have supplied its characteristic teachings. It is not clear whether the Messianism of the Jewish Christians was combined with a conscious and pronounced theology of creation; but, in any case, the Holy

[1] Cp. S. Mowinckel, *Han Som Kommer*, p. 262.
[2] Cp. especially Col. i. 16; John i. 1–14; Heb. i. 2, 10.
[3] Dodd, *The Apostolic Preaching and its Developments*, pp. 28 ff.
[4] T. W. Manson, *op. cit.*, p. 252.

Scriptures were the common property of Jews and Christians, and supplied them with a single conception of the world and of its creator. The crucial issue is how far Christology was stated within the limits of Old Testament imagery, and whether the statement involved a remoulding of this imagery. Christology must take into account the various forms of later Jewish Messianism, for Jesus Himself accepts them as His own. But in so far as He had a Messianic ideal, it is clear that He stated it in His own special way.

The Synoptic presentation of Jesus was intended to show that He had difficulty in replacing traditional Messianic ideas by His own individual teaching even among His most intimate disciples. Jesus's own Messianic teaching was determined by the idea of vicarious suffering. The disciples were led to accept this idea unconditionally only by the events of Good Friday. Unless Jesus had Himself spoken of the suffering of the Messiah, Christianity could never have existed; this at least is clear. If Jesus made vicarious suffering the central feature of His Messianic teaching, it is reasonable to suppose that His especial source was the Suffering Servant imagery of Deutero-Isaiah.

We must return to the distinction between two forms of eschatological teaching suggested by T. W. Manson. The second of these is stated to have its origin in Deutero-Isaiah, when he regards the task of the elect people as the endurance of vicarious suffering on behalf of the Gentiles. This implies a far-reaching though not absolute universalism bound up with the monotheism of these prophecies. The peculiar concern of Deutero-Isaiah with the theology of creation is surely no mere coincidence. His prophecies are based on unconditional monotheism, on an extensive universalism, on the ktisiology which corresponds to these two principles, and finally on a soteriology expressed in terms of vicarious suffering.

Jesus's own teaching must be understood in such terms as these. We shall not here discuss at length the image of the Son of Man; we merely notice that Jesus alludes to Daniel, but makes no very considerable reference to the ideas first

known to us from the Book of Enoch.[1]   Here, as in general,
Jesus goes to the Holy Scriptures without being considerably
influenced by contemporary religious views.   He goes right
back to the root and foundation of the doctrines which he
teaches.[2]   There is little more in common between Enoch
and the teaching of Jesus than the image of the Son of Man
stated in terms of the Heavenly Man.   Jesus gives this
image, which he gets from Daniel, a totally new meaning
by fusing it with another scriptural image, the Suffering
Servant of Isaiah liii.[3]   We would say one thing very clearly,
however.   It is usual nowadays to emphasize that Jesus as
the Son of Man is not just a human being, but the Heavenly
Man.   We must not overlook the process by which these
associations of meaning are built up.   The term "the Son
of Man" as a Messianic title retained some of its shades
of meaning in the Old Testament.   The Son of Man is an
individual of man as a species (see especially Ps. viii. 5, which
is interpreted Christologically in Heb. ii. 6 ff.), and the
species is created in the image of God.   In the Old Testament anyone can be called a "Son of Man"; in the New
Testament there is only one Son of Man, Jesus Christ, who
is also called in a Christological sense the image of God
(2 Cor. iv. 4).   Christ is the New Man, the Second Adam; as
Son of Man, He is also the perfect man.   What is said in the
Old Testament about all men in general is reserved in the
New Testament for the one Son of Man.[4]

[1] We should notice, however, the opinion of Mowinckel that Dan. vii. 13–14
and 1 Enoch xxxi.–lxxi. have a common background.   He holds that the
image of the Son of Man in Daniel is a symbol of the Holy People, *i.e.* Israel,
but in Enoch bears its supposedly original sense of the Heavenly Man.

[2] Compare also his controversy with the Pharisees concerning divorce
(Matt. xix. 8).   Here Jesus argues from the principle *ap' arches*.   A similar
point is made by E. Hoskyns and F. Noel Davey, *The Riddle of the New Testament*,
p. 140: "Jesus, then, cannot be fitted into contemporary Judaism; he goes
behind it to the Law and the Prophets and definitely states that now is the time
of their fulfilment."

[3] Rudolf Otto, in *Reich Gottes und Menschensohn* (1934), rightly suggests that
the synthesis of the image of the Son of Man and the Suffering Servant is
original in the teaching of Jesus.

[4] Compare the imagery of 1 Enoch and the comments of Mowinckel, *Han
Som Kommer*, p. 250.   We may notice that the image of the Son of Man and the
story of Adam have different roots, but the New Testament apparently combines
them.

On the basis of Jesus's own Messianic teaching, the Christology of the Primitive Church developed as one might have expected in a Palestinian environment. Christological speculation had an early origin; so-called "cosmic Christology" was not a later, Pauline development. St Paul met with it in Christian circles from the beginning; he did not adopt a Christianity whose Messianism was crude and primitive. The Christology of the Apostolic Age was faithful in detail to Jesus's own teaching, which we have already outlined.[1]

Thus, in Jewish Christianity in Palestine, Christological dogma developed from Jesus's own teaching. And on this point there is no discrepancy between Jesus and Jewish Christianity on the one hand and Pauline Christianity on the other. The only point at which Jewish Christianity differed from Gentile was in its attitude to the Law. The Jewish Christian deviation is puzzling, for Pauline Christianity undoubtedly saw the real intention of Jesus's original teaching about the Law. Perhaps St Peter's attitude to the Gentiles was influenced by ideas derived from Ezekiel, to which reference has been made; nevertheless, he seems to have been open to the acceptance of some kind of universalist thought.[2]

Pauline Christianity held as steadfastly to the Old Testament as Palestinian, and the two may be said to harmonize at all main points. There are formal differences, but Paul was true to the traditions which he received; he did not hellenize Christianity. Further, he interpreted the Gospel of Jesus faithfully in matters of ktisiology; his presentation of Jesus as the Second Adam, for example, corresponds to Jesus's self-proclamation as the Son of Man.

We shall therefore proceed to assert two things. 1. The

[1] Cp. Frederick C. Grant, *An Introduction to New Testament Thought* (1950), p. 35: "The Christology with which Paul began his career . . . was the more advanced Christology which lies at the basis of the Marcan formulation (or reformulation) of the traditions of Jesus's ministry of healing and teaching."

[2] See Anton Fridrichsen, "The Apostle and his Message", in *Inbjudning till doktorspromotionen i Uppsala*, 1947.

New Testament presupposes the Old.[1]   The teaching of the Old Testament concerning monotheism, universalism and ktisiology is continued in the New.   2. The novel thing that distinguishes the New Testament from the Old is its Christology.   It is, however, no arbitrary supplement; it is built on the fundamental conceptions of the Old Testament, and foreshadowed in the imagery of Adam, the Son of Man, the Holy Remnant, the Servant of the Lord, and the like, which is reborn in New Testament Christology.

The influence of later Jewish religious ideas could only be estimated if the New Testament material was fully analysed.   The crucial question is, however, whether developed Judaism is the bridge between the Old and New Testaments, or whether Jesus reverted directly to the Old Testament in conscious reaction and protest against the whole of intermediate and contemporary Jewish religion. I should attempt an answer on these lines.   It is not accurate to say that Judaism, as represented by the Apocrypha and Pseudepigrapha, is the bridge between the Old and New Testaments;   this is a misleading metaphor.[2]   I would rather describe it as the background against which New Testament images are shaped on Old Testament models. For instance, Enoch gave definition to the idea of the Son of Man, but not in the New Testament sense.[3]   Jesus knew the term in current language, but He gave it a new meaning in the light of His own unique mission by associating with it such Old Testament images as the Suffering Servant.   This is generally true of the eschatological ideas in Jewish apocalyptic writings; although there are some things in them which have no parallel in the Old Testament but which appear in the New, for example in Pauline Christology.[4]

[1] This may seem a truism, but recent discussions have invested it with a new and richer meaning.   See especially the already cited books of E. Hoskyns and F. Noel Davey, and of Frederick C. Grant.
[2] We would not disparage the importance of Rabbinic literature for the understanding of the New Testament; it is not relevant to our thesis at this point.
[3] A good analysis of the idea of the Son of Man in Enoch is given by Erik Sjöberg in his book *Der Menschensohn im Äthiopischen Henochbuch*, 1946.
[4] S. Mowinckel gives examples in his *Han Som Kommer*.

It is an over-simplification to say that the Christology of the New Testament has grown organically in the soil of Old Testament ideas. The New Testament is not just a commentary on the Old; it is authentically new and original. It contains many bold reinterpretations of the older theology. We may instance the use of Psalm cii in Hebrews i. 10, which is part of a Christological passage:

Thou, LORD, in the beginning hast laid the foundations
of the earth,
And the heavens are the works of thy hands:
They shall perish; but thou continuest:
And they all shall wax old as doth a garment;
And as a mantle shalt thou roll them up,
As a garment, and they shall be changed:
But thou art the same, and thy years shall not fail.
(Ps. cii. 24–27.)

This psalm is related by the writer to the Hebrews to the historical man, Jesus of Nazareth. This is possible because the New Testament bears witness that Christ is the centre; Christology is everywhere its ultimate subject-matter.

Oscar Cullmann has shown that the earliest Christian credal affirmations quoted in the New Testament are Christological.[1] If they have a double form, the actions of the Father and the Son are paralleled, so that the creative works of the Father and the Son are compared. This is further evidence of the unity of the New Testament.

New Testament Christology has then two outstanding doctrines: faith in Jesus as the Son of God in a unique sense, and faith in him as the Son of Man in the sense his own teaching gave to the phrase, both individualizing it and transmuting it through association with suffering. It would perhaps be going too far to deny any internal development in the Christology of the New Testament, when due regard is had to the synoptic tradition of the words and works of Jesus. There is a very great distance between our Lord's solitary prayer in Gethsemane and the Son through which the

[1] See *Die ersten Christlichen Glaubensbekenntnisse* (*Theol. Studien. Eine Schriftreihe hrsg. von Karl Barth*, 15, 1943).

worlds were created in Hebrews. But the author of Hebrews is conscious of the paradox, and boldly proclaims that He through whom heaven and earth were created was really incarnate in Jesus of Nazareth, the crucified Jew. We must insist on the fact that the New Testament writers recognized the paradox, and if that is borne in mind, the development which we acknowledge in New Testament Christology will stand in a different light. It was the development of a paradox; but the paradox was in the facts.

As a mere formulation or association of ideas, the New Testament doctrine of the Messiah was not particularly paradoxical or offensive on grounds of novelty. It was partially anticipated in Judaism. Using only ideas which are domestic to Judaism, we can construct a synthetic figure which is recognizably similar to the glorified Christ of the New Testament, so long as the Passion is left out of account. But once this synthetic figure is related to the life and death of Jesus of Nazareth the apparent similarity vanishes. The kind of Christology that one might build up from such Jewish ideas as the Heavenly Man would be utterly abstract and imaginary; Judaism could never allow the combination of such ideas with an historical event. The Incarnation, with its wealth of significance for ktisiology, was bound to create its own new system of religious belief and practice.

The fact of the Crucifixion made faith in Christ a *scandalon* to the Jews. But Jesus had already proved a *scandalon* to them before his death. What relation is there between the *scandalon* before the cross and the *scandalon* of the cross? This is one way of stating the principal riddle of the New Testament, for faith in Jesus before the Crucifixion and faith in the risen and ascended Christ merge into each other. The Resurrection as an isolated fact did not create Christology; it supplied convincing proof to the disciples that Jesus was the Christ as they already believed. Had there not been faith in Christ before the cross, there could have been none afterwards.

If Christology is thus central to the New Testament, and

19

if the whole of the Old Testament is made explicit in the New, there must have been a fundamental reinterpretation of Holy Scripture in order to establish a real unity between the two Testaments. The Gospels state the reason for the reinterpretation. It was not a mere speculation, for no speculation could have set in motion so drastic a process; it was an historical event. After all, there was plenty of speculation in Judaism, if speculation was sufficient. Only the historical reality of the Incarnation could achieve the revolution.

If Christ is the centre of the New Testament, the theology of Creation, which was of such importance to the Old, must have been interpreted Christologically. That is why, as we have seen, Christ could be described in the words of a psalm addressed to the Creator of all things.

v

Mosaic religion centred on the election and the covenant; thus, it possessed the characteristic feature of later Yahwism, in that it was an historical religion. When the old, pre-Canaanite religion became subject to the influence of Canaanite cults, the typical Israelite El-religion arose. There was a period of syncretism.[1] Yahweh-El became a high god of the general near-Eastern type. As such, he was the Creator-God, and the Creation became a central theme of religious life and thought through the cult. This kind of ktisiology is, however, naturalistic rather than historical. Creation is thought of in terms of a cyclical process of renewal in nature.

With reformist prophetism a new era began in religious thinking. History counterbalanced nature, and the ethical and personal factor assumed a predominant importance. A fresh experience of the true nature of God brought about this change. The increasingly clear insight that God is one,

[1] See Ivan Engnell, *Gamla Testamenket, En traditionshistorisk inledning* (1945), pp. 135 ff.

just and almighty widened the horizon and modified the content of religious belief. The histories of the Creation and of the elect people were related to each other. Ktisiology was, so to speak, historized, and the work of creation became an act of election. God made a covenant with the first man, created in his image, and in the very manner of his creation lay man's dignity and value. Ethical thinking found its determining themes in ktisiology.

Akin to the conception of the dignity of man were the universalist ideas of one God and one humanity, and these too were seen as part of ktisiology; though we have noticed the difficulties which beset universalism in Hebrew thought, and its failure to find full expression before the Incarnation. Only when the Old Testament conception of the people of God was radically transformed could there be a thorough-going universalism. Yet when this was established in Christ, there was nothing there that was not implicit in the absolute monotheism of Deutero-Isaiah.

The transformation of the nationalistic conception of the people of God was prepared by the prophets through the idea of the Holy Remnant. The difficult ideas of the Suffering Servant and the Son of Man belong to the same circle of thought. Because of its intrinsic variety, the development of eschatology in Jewish religion can be explained in several ways. S. Mowinckel has suggested that eschatology arose from the cult. This seems probable, in view of the Messianic bearing of Jewish eschatology. But the developed eschatology in some parts of the Book of Isaiah and in the later apocryphal writings cannot, as I believe, be explained without reference to the ethical experience of the prophets, and their consequent attempt to interpret the history of Israel and of mankind. A sense of sin and injustice is the salient feature of Jewish eschatology and the theology of the new creation; and eschatology in its most significant form is always related to ktisiology.

We are nowadays convinced that the Gospel must be understood eschatologically. That conviction would of itself lead us to treat the widespread presence of a ktisiological pattern in the New Testament as a working hypothesis. We have now shown that there is plenty of particular evidence to confirm it. New Testament Christology, like Old Testament Messianism, is patently eschatological. The Lord as the Son of God and the Son of Man is the Second Adam (1 Cor. xv. 45) or, as we might say in current language, the eschatological Adam. He bears the image of God (2 Cor. iv. 5), and he is the New Man (Col. iii. 9 ff.). He is *monogenēs, prōtotocos, archē.* In Christ there is a new creation (2 Cor. v. 17).

Through the Second Adam, God makes a new covenant with man. The New Testament also contains the idea of an elect people of God; but this new people is not restricted to the old Israel. By inward faith, everyone can become a member of the people of God. In the Old Testament, the idea of the people of God was an obstacle to the full establishment of universalism based on faith in the Creator-God. In the New Testament, universalism is made possible by the idea of the new people of God.

The Old Testament supplied the New with a ktisiology but it could not solve the problem of eschatology. This is made clear by the tension between universalism and particularism that even Deutero-Isaiah could not resolve. An entirely new answer to the eschatological problem was required, and this is what the New Testament provided. Our Lord was not just a Jewish Messiah and cannot be represented as such. The Jews themselves have never had any doubt on that score. The name of Christ is only formally the same as Messiah; in meaning, it is a new word which must be understood in terms of the reborn images of the Son of Man, the Son of God and the last Adam. Jesus himself preferred the title Son of Man, and filled it with new meaning. He thus ascribed to himself a unique position in the history of mankind as the New Man, through whom all creation will be restored as in the beginning. The New Testament writers presented their Christology in this way.

I hope to discuss the subject-matter of this essay more fully in my forthcoming monograph.

II

THE IDEA OF GOD'S PEOPLE IN THE BIBLE

G. A. Danell

THE CONCEPTION of a people chosen by God can only be understood in the light of belief in one God. It has indeed been asserted in various quarters that the monotheistic conception of God, as such, was established in Israel, perhaps by the so-called "scriptural" prophets in the eighth and seventh centuries, perhaps by Deutero-Isaiah in the sixth century, or perhaps even later still, and that the original Mosaic religion was a so-called monolatry, or practical monotheism. Because Yahweh is only one, although the mightiest, among many gods, the character of the Election and of the Covenant must be different from what it would be if He were the only God. As Chemosh is the god of Moab and Milcom the god of Ammon, so Yahweh is the God of Israel, making an exclusive claim to the worship and obedience of His people. Further, in power He is distinguished from other gods by His jealousy, His *qin'ah*, which will not permit any other god but Him in Israel. Under such circumstances Israel does not take an absolutely unique position among the nations, and has only a relative advantage in that Yahweh is jealous and exclusive and is mightier than other gods, and so can conquer them and their nations, and can excite terror among the neighbours of Israel (Ex. xv. 14 ff., xxiii. 27 ff.; Deut. xi. 25; Josh. ii. 9 f.).

But if the question is regarded not from the evolutionist point of view of the history of religion but from that of Biblical theology, the problem is not to reconstruct a religious development which has left certain traces behind in the Old Testament Scriptures in spite of the dogmatic revision they have undergone. It is to find and describe the basic thought of the canonical books; and it is clear that the question must be seen against the background of true monotheism. Still, the difference between monolatry and monotheism must not be exaggerated, because monolatry also involves a god of a universal and monotheistic nature, a "high" god, a god of heaven and of creation.[1]

Even if it is possible in the Old Testament Scriptures to trace a development or a progressive revelation from a relatively unreflecting monolatry to a more theologically elaborated monotheism, it is quite clear that the Old Testament as a whole, in its present condition, represents a monotheistic position. This is undoubtedly the case even in the Pentateuch, in which may be studied the development and meaning of Election.

The call of Abraham and the Election of the people of Israel are described and set in a universal context. There is not one god amongst many who creates a cult-congregation, but the one God, Creator of heaven and earth, who chooses one people from the many on earth which He has Himself created. The Election and the foundation of God's own people must be seen against the background of Creation and of the whole prehistory in Genesis i–xi. The God who created heaven and earth and mankind, who replenished the earth and divided it among many peoples, is the same God who chooses Abraham and Isaac.

Not only the Creation, but also the Fall of Man, forms the background of the Election. If we do not recognize this, we cannot understand the special significance of the Election and the idea of God's people which it implies. There is clearly an interior theological relation between them. God created man in His own image and commanded him to replenish the earth and subdue it. The whole of God's Creation was good in the beginning, and this included man; but through the Fall, man was corrupted and with him the whole of Creation. He fell so deeply into sin that God at last had to destroy the whole of mankind, except eight persons, through the Flood. But even then, mankind which, through Noah, was saved from the Flood was corrupt.

[1] Cf. Engnell, *Gamla Testamentet* I., p. 110 f.

Genesis xi. records the unsuccessful attempt of men, by themselves and in their own power, to gather themselves into a unity in order to make themselves a *name* (*shem*). In the following chapter this has a parallel in the story of how Yahweh called Abraham out of his own country with the promise to make of him a great nation, to make his *name* (*shem*) great and to make him a blessing. Yahweh founds a new centre on earth, an antithesis to Babel, around which all the nations of the earth are to be united: "and in thee shall all families of the earth be blessed" (or "bless themselves").

It is difficult to deny that the position of the account of Abraham's call immediately after that of the tower of Babel is more than accidental; a contrast between them is certainly intended. There is a positive parallel to the account of the Fall and its consequences. In both cases *pride* is the motive of men's action; in both cases God frustrates their plans and prevents their securing a power like His own by their own efforts; in both cases God gives a promise to them shortly afterwards, and ultimately effects the re-establishment of mankind—after the Fall in the words about the seed of the woman, and after the fall of Babel in the calling and blessing of Abraham. In both cases there is a new beginning from God's side, against the background of the unsuccessful expedients of man and of the straits in which they left him.

Through a series of decrees and acts of Election, Yahweh creates the people which He promised to Abraham. The idea of a remnant is implied in that of Election. The people of God is established out of a remnant, even if this expression does not occur in the text. The ancestor, Abraham, was *one* man, who went into exile at Yahweh's call and from him the people was descended (cp. Ezek. xxxiii. 24; Isa. li. 1–3).

Even the theme "from death to life" occurs in the accounts of Abraham. When he and his wife were both come to old age and were as dead, through a divine miracle there was born to them a son who should inherit the blessing (cp. Rom. iv. 16 ff.; Heb. xi. 11).

Not Ishmael the elder but Isaac the younger, not Esau

but his younger twin brother Jacob inherits the blessing. And among the sons of Jacob, Joseph, rather than his elder half-brothers, is the bearer of the blessing. Yahweh is with him to make him successful in everything, even during his misfortunes, in order to make him the saviour of his family. The blessing radiates from him, so that his brothers become partakers of it.

It is clear that Joseph too illustrates the "remnant" motif which appears so clearly in the scriptural Prophets, and the parallel with the time of Babylonian Exile is striking. The son in exile constitutes the new beginning through which the family is saved and renewed in order to grow into a great people. The way to renewal passes through death to life.

Another "remnant" was Israel in Egypt, a people, "the fewest of all people", which Yahweh made into His *own people* (Deut. vii. 6 ff.). In this time of need Israel is saved by Moses, also a man *in exile*, who gives his people a new beginning. In the fight against Pharaoh, Yahweh appears principally as the Lord of all the world, conquering the mightiest nation on earth, by means of His power over the elements. When he called Israel His first-born son (Ex. iv. 22) he implied that other nations also belong to Him. This idea is more clearly expressed in the song of Moses (Deut. xxxii. 8) : "When the Most-High (*Elyon*) divided the nations (*goyim*), when He separated mankind by setting the bounds of the peoples ('*ammim*) [1] according to the number of the sons of God (so in LXX; M.T. the sons of Israel), then His people, Jacob, became the lot of Yahweh's inheritance and Israel, the lot of His inheritance." (So in LXX.) Nyberg sees in these verses a proof of the original subordination of Yahweh to Elyon, who divides the nations among the sons of God, of which Yahweh is one. [2]

This is not, however, true of the Song as a whole in its present form, where Yahweh appears as the one true God (v. 39) and the rest of the gods are called demons (*shedim*)

[1] Cf. Acts xvii. 26.
[2] *Studien zum Religionskampf im Alten Testament*, A.R.W. 35 (1938), p. 366.

and non-gods (v. 17, 21).[1] It is usual here as elsewhere in the Old Testament (*e.g.* Gen. xiv. 22; Num. xxiv. 16; Ps. xci. 1) to identify Elyon with Yahweh. He is the Ruler of all the nations and has chosen Israel-Jacob as the special lot of His inheritance. This universal character of Yahweh, and the distinct position of Israel among the nations as a consequence of the Election, is an important theme of the Balaam songs. Balaam from Aram is forced by Yahweh-Elohim-Elyon-Shaddai to bless His people Israel, whose unique status is strongly emphasized: "the people shall dwell alone and shall not be reckoned among the (other) nations" (Num. xxiii. 9).

As the Election in the story of Moses presupposes that Yahweh is a universal, creative God, the one true God, so the Election has itself a universal purpose. When Yahweh speaks to Moses about Israel before the Covenant, He says, "If ye will obey my voice indeed and keep my Covenant then ye shall be a peculiar treasure unto me above all people: *for all the earth is mine:* and ye shall be unto me a kingdom of priests and an holy nation" (Ex. xix. 5 f.). Israel thus occupies a distinct position with the God who is the Lord of all the earth, and its position amongst the nations corresponds to that which is occupied by the Levites among the tribes of Israel. In Israel, Levi is the tribe of priests and Yahweh's special inheritance among the tribes. In the same way Israel is the priestly people, Yahweh's own people. The Levites belong to Yahweh as the ransom of all the first-born of the children of Israel (Num. iii. 12–13, viii. 14–18). All the first-born among men and animals are, strictly speaking, the property of Yahweh (Ex. xiii. 11–16). As the substitute for the first-born of Israel, the tribe of Levi

---

[1] See Albright, *From the Stone Age to Christianity,* pp. 22 ff. Cf. Ps. cvi. 37 ff.; 1 Cor. viii. 4 ff., x. 19 ff.; Apoc. ix. 20. As for the meaning of these terms, see E. Langton, *Essentials of Demonology* (1949), pp. 16 ff., 51 f.

From the point of view of religious phenomenology we have here an example of the degradation of hostile gods to the status of demons. From the point of view of Bible theology it is an expression of dualistic monotheism: over against the one God there stand hostile spirits. "Non-gods" here probably does not mean non-existence but only the denial of their being gods. The Egyptians are also said to be "non-gods" but they ended as men (Isa. xxxi. 3).

to some extent occupies the position of the first-born of the tribes of Israel, even if this is never directly stated. This reminds us of the position of Israel as the first-born among the nations of the earth (Ex. iv. 22). The comparison with the priestly tribe of Levi shows how the *holiness* of Israel is to be understood. As the priestly people of the earth, it is separated from other nations in order to be Yahweh's special people, but this separation evidently has a universal purpose. As there are laws about the holiness of the priests (Lev. xxi), so there are laws for the holiness of the Israelites which are not demanded of the rest of the nations (Lev. xix). As the Levites do service in the tabernacle and make atonement for the whole of Israel (Num. viii. 19), so the special task of Israel among the nations of the earth is to render to Yahweh, the one true God, the worship and obedience which He can rightly claim from all the nations He has created. Thus Yahweh says about Abraham, "For I know him, that he will command his children and his household after him, and they shall keep the way of the Lord, to do justice and judgment" (Gen. xviii. 19), on another occasion, "The Lord Thy God He is the God (*ha 'elohim*), the faithful God" (Deut. vii. 9), and again, "Thou shalt therefore keep the commandments and the statutes and the judgments which I command thee this day to do them" (v. 11). Against the background of the Fall and of its result in the apostasy of the whole of mankind from the true God, the meaning and purpose of the Election is clear: God chooses one people to be His own in order that it may worship Him and live according to His commandments. God created man in His image, but man apostasized through his disobedience. The chosen people is to be like God in holiness. "Ye shall be holy, for I the Lord your God am holy" (Lev. xix. 2).

The immediate consequence of the Election and the Covenant is seen in Yahweh's fight for His people, in which he conquers their enemies and gives them dominion over the Promised Land. Yahweh's war is Israel's war and *vice versa*. It is impossible to deny the particular conditions; the horizon is undoubtedly limited. But the solidarity of Yahweh

28

with His people is never without condition. Stipulations are, on the contrary, made from the very beginning. If Israel breaks the conditions of the Covenant, it is punished, but if it performs its stipulated duties, then Yahweh's faithfulness is absolutely steadfast, and He gives His people blessing, success and prosperity in peace and in war. The so-called Deuteronomic historical revision has, as we know, applied this idea throughout the history of Israel until its exile. The one great exception to the rule is the tragic death of the pious King Josiah, which is quite contrary to the official theory. The thing most effective to modern minds in Yahweh's relation to His chosen people is the *ḥerem* principle, that no mercy is allowed towards a conquered enemy. Yahweh's war is total war, which demands the complete annihilation of conquered nations. This principle is energetically maintained by some of the most important representatives of strict Yahwism, *e.g.* Moses, Joshua and Samuel. But the motive which lies behind it is obvious. Yahweh is a jealous God (*'el qanna*), who does not allow any god but Himself in the Israelite cult. Foreign nations tempt Israel to worship their gods, and because of that any mixing with them is prohibited. The *ḥerem* is part of Yahweh's fight against the idols. Yahweh's war must be set against the background of the first commandment. The war against foreign nations is essentially war against their gods, which are no true gods. Yahweh's war is in fact the same as that proclaimed in the beginning between the seed of the serpent and the seed of the woman. This is clear, since Hvidberg has shown that the serpent in Paradise represents the god of fruitfulness, Baal.[1] Yahweh's war is a fight to gain dominion on earth through His instrument, Israel; the narrow and intolerant particularism is brought into a wider relation with an implicitly universal aim. Israel's war becomes part of the war for the existence of the Kingdom of God on earth and for a right knowledge and worship of the one true God.

This approach is also to be adopted when seeking to

[1] Cf. Ringgren, *Svensk Exegetisk Årsbok*, xiii. (1948), pp. 13, 40.

understand the word "enemy" in the Psalms and the narrow particularism of the post-exilic period of Ezra and Nehemiah. The value of this particularism is that it consolidates the position of the Kingdom of God, and promotes pure faith in God. In spite of its interim character in the Divine economy, it receives an absolute meaning; its universal aim is never quite obscured, but is implicit in it.

This underlying "universalist" idea is clearly expressed in some of the Biblical Prophets. Universalism is part of the vision of the future which expects the re-establishment of Paradise (Isa. ii. 2–4; Mic. iv. 1–5; Isa. xi). But it is characteristic that this world peace is a "pax Israelitica"; it will be established with Jerusalem as its centre, with the son of David as its leader, and consequently will be under the supremacy of Israel. From one point of view it is possible to say that "particularism" is thus brought to its climax, since Israel is the imperial nation on earth which rules and is served by all other nations on earth (Isa. ix; Zech. ix. 9–17). If we remember the character of Yahweh's war as described in the historical books, the result is evidently final victory for the nation of Israel. It is Yahweh, the one true God, who, through His people Israel, will reign over all the nations on earth. The supremacy is therefore not based on mere external surrender; there are also hints that all nations shall come to know and worship God through Israel. This is clearly stated in the already quoted reference, Isaiah ii. 2–4: "All nations (*goyim*) shall flow to Jerusalem and say: 'Come ye, and let us go up to the mountain of the Lord, to the House of the God of Jacob, and He will teach us of His ways and we will walk in His paths; for out of Zion shall go forth the Law and the word of the Lord from Jerusalem'."

In the *ʿebed-Yahweh* songs the same idea is expressed. The Servant of Yahweh, representing Israel, will be a light to the Gentiles (Isa. xlii. 6, xlv. 22, xlix. 6). The universal character of Israel's vocation is most clearly expressed by Deutero-Isaiah (*e.g.* Isa. li. 4), and is undoubtedly closely connected with his strong emphasis on Yahweh as the God of the whole earth (Isa. liv. 5) and as the one living God. But here as always Zion-Jerusalem, representing Israel-Jacob, is at the centre (xliv. 26–28, xlv. 13, lii. 2, 8).[1]

Israel's national destiny and the final aim of the Election are thus quite clearly universal in the prophetic Scriptures; but this revelation of the future is, as we know, very closely linked with the announcement of a severe judgement. That the prophetic judgement is derived from the idea of the Election of God's people, and is the more severe because of it, is clear from Amos iii. 2: "You only have I known of all the families of the earth, therefore I will punish you for all your iniquities." The same tendency is also found in Isaiah ii, where the revelation of the promise carries with it a threat of punishment (ii. 5 ff.). The Election is the often unexpressed but always evident basis of every prophecy of judgement; it heightens the claim on Israel, and results in a correspondingly harder punishment. The Prophets do not suggest that Israel is more evil than other nations; its sin consists primarily in not living up to its peculiar position and of desiring to be like other nations: "We will be as the heathen (*goyim*), as the families of the countries, to serve wood and stone" (Ezek. xx. 32). Because of the Election, and of its own peculiar position as God's own people, Israel is more sinful than other nations and its guilt is greater than theirs in worshipping their gods and imitating their deeds. The whole purpose of the Election is ineffective when Israel relies on its consequent solidarity with Yahweh, but breaks His commandments. Just because of this, the punishment had to come to make it possible for Yahweh to create a people after his own heart out of this backsliding Israel. The judgement which is pronounced is no doubt of a root-and-branch sort, but it never aims at total annihilation. It is a *catharsis* aiming at renewal and resurrection through death to life. The idea of the remnant is consequently a necessary part of the prophetic announcement of judgement and connects it organically to the promise.

[1] That the religion of Israel is *both* universal *and* national, particularly in Deutero-Isaiah, is emphasized by Engnell, *op. cit.*, p. 159 f.

Estimates of the actual extent of the remnant vary during different periods. The conception itself is present even where the word is not expressly mentioned. It is thus quite obvious that in Jerusalemic tradition the tribe of Judah, which alone remained under the House of David after the rebellion of Jeroboam, was the remnant containing in itself the seed of the future. In 2 Chronicles x. this is quite evident. It also seems probable that the prophet Isaiah, in the beginning, conceived Judah as the remnant, the tenth (Isa. vi. 13) [1] which should return to Yahweh (vii. 3), even if he soon concluded that this remnant too would have to be reduced (vi. 13). It is probable that Judah, after the destruction of the kingdom of Israel, and still more after the campaign of Sennacherib against Jerusalem, regarded itself as the remnant and as having undergone the predicted judgement; but all those hopes were inexorably denounced by Jeremiah in his announcements of a further judgement. Both he and his great contemporary Ezekiel fix their hopes on the exiles in Babylon. This *golah* is indicated as the Remnant from which the future Israel will grow. Once more the way to life and renewal passes through death and destruction. The Jews returning from the Exile regard themselves as the remnant, but it is significant that it is never possible exactly to identify the remnant with any visible and actual embodiment. The whole of visible Israel is never the same as the true Israel; there are always many ungodly among the people.

The idea of the remnant has a Messianic significance, for example in the prophecy of Emmanuel in Isaiah vii. and xi. Israel as resuscitated from the remnant will be ruled by a son of David, and the Messianic Figure himself is described as the remnant out of which the new people springs. He is the new rod of the stem of Jesse, the branch of its roots (Isa. xi. 1); and this is very close to the expression of the "holy seed" (Isa. vi. 13), which signifies the remnant. He is also called ṣemaḥ, the Branch (growing out from the roots, Jer. xxiii. 5,

---

[1] Cf. Danell, *Studies in the Name Israel in the O.T.*, p. 167; Engnell, *The Call of Isaiah*, p. 51.

xxxiii. 15), and this title is used by Zechariah, probably of Zerubbabel (Zech. iii. 8, vi. 12). This movement between individual and collective is a well-known peculiarity of the Semitic mind. These considerations explain the change between individual and collective in the so-called '*ebed-Yahweh* songs. Personally I believe that the servant is an individual,[1] and the name Israel, identified with the Servant (Isa. xlix. 3), is to be explained in this way. But the identity of the Servant and Israel becomes still clearer in view of the close relationship between the Messiah and the Remnant which I have just mentioned. The idea of the remnant explains why the Servant of Jahveh, in certain passages, has a clearly collective character and represents the whole of Israel (Isa. xlii. 18 ff., xliii. 10, xliv. 1 ff.), while in the so-called '*ebed-Yahweh* songs he is obviously an individual. The Servant-Messiah is the true Israel, the Remnant, concentrated in one person, and also the One who will re-establish the scattered people and draw all nations into the worship of Yahweh.

Even though the terminology in Isaiah liii. 2 is different from that in Isaiah vi. 13, xi. 1, and Jeremiah xxiii. 5, xxxiii. 15 (*joneq, shoresh*), the relationship is still so strong that there may be a direct allusion to these Messianic passages.[2] This would confirm my view that the Servant is identical with the Remnant, the new beginning of the re-established Israel. The way is the same as it has always been, and is expressed in terms of the doctrine of the Remnant as a passing through death to life. It might be said that the idea of God's people in the Old Testament culminates in the person of the Servant, who is the idea of the Remnant personified as an individual.

Parallel to this line of thought is another conception, that of the new Covenant (Jer. xxxi. 31 ff. Cp. Ezek. xi. 19 ff., xxxvi. 26 ff.). This is closely associated with the Servant, as the Servant of Yahweh will Himself be the covenant of the

---

[1] Cf. Nyberg, *Svensk Exegetisk Årsbok* 7 (1949), pp. 25–89; Engnell, "The 'ebed Yahweh Songs and the Suffering Messiah in Deutero-Isaiah" (*Bull. John Ryl. Libr.*, 1948); North, *The Suffering Servant in Deutero-Isaiah* (1948).
[2] Cf. Engnell, *op. cit.*, p. 31.

C

people (*b^erith-'am*, Isa. xlii. 6, xlix. 8). That this covenant, represented by the Servant, is the same as the new covenant announced by Jeremiah, seems very likely when we consider how forcibly Deutero-Isaiah announces the *new* thing which Yahweh shall perform (Isa. xliii. 19). It can scarcely be too audacious to use Isaiah liii in explaining the meaning of *b^erith-'am*. Through the passion and death of the Servant the New Covenant, the covenant of the people, is inaugurated.[1] He is the Sacrificial Lamb whose blood is the seal of the New Covenant, effecting the new creation of Israel. In this way Yahweh seeks to accomplish His work for Israel, and to give its people a new mind of obedience to His will. The universal purpose will also be revealed and the Servant will transcend national limitations and become a light to the Gentiles (Isa. xlii. 6, xlix. 6), bearing the sins of many (Isa. liii. 12). So the Old Testament reaches its climax and the idea of God's people its full elaboration.

The relevance to the New Testament of the idea of God's people in the Old Testament will only be dealt with here in a summary and tentative way. A number of lines of thought are carried on from the Old Testament and appear side by side. In particular, the theology of the New Testament presupposes the Creation and the Fall. The fact of salvation proclaimed in it is to be understood against the background of the following elementary facts: man created by God is fallen and bound by sin; God therefore creates a new humanity in Christ; Christ is the New Man, the Original Man, the Son of Man, the new Adam. Presumably the genealogy in Luke suggests this by tracing His ancestors back to Adam; but the theology of the Second Adam is more fully developed by St Paul in Romans v. 12 ff., 1 Corinthians xv. 20 ff. and 45 ff., and also underlies the expression to "put off the old man and put on the new man, which after God is created in righteousness and true holiness" (Eph. iv. 22 ff. Cp. Col. iii. 9 f.). Through Christ, God re-establishes fallen man and re-creates him in His image, according to the divine image in Christ. This new mankind

[1] Cf. Engnell, *op. cit.*, p. 38.

34

is born into eternal life through baptism, passing *through death to life*.

But Christ is not only the second Adam; God does not pass over the whole history of the people of Israel in order to revert directly to the very beginning. Christ is also the fulfilment of the promises to Israel and the perfection of all those "Saviour-persons" who had gone before Him in the sacred history. He is the son of Abraham and also the son of David (Matt. i. 1), the two great bearers of the Promise in the Old Testament. St Matthew, in his genealogy, traces His ancestors back to Abraham, and tries to illustrate the subject which St Paul deals with more fully in his letter to the Galatians. The gist of this letter can be stated as follows. Who really belong to the true Israel, the people of God? Who are the sons of Abraham, partaking in his blessing? The answer is, Those who, like Abraham, believe in His promises; but they are the sons of Abraham not merely by physical descent but in a real sacramental way. Christ is the *Seed* (iii. 16), the Bearer of the Promises and blessings. "For ye are all the children of God by faith in Christ Jesus, *for as many of you as have been baptised into Christ have put on Christ*." "If ye be Christ, *then are ye Abraham's seed*, and heirs according to the Promise" (iii. 29). Thus the new Israel is created, God's Israel (iii. 16), breaking national bounds, there being "neither Jew nor Greek, neither bond nor free, neither male nor female" (iii. 28). Christ is thus the head of Israel, in and through whom citizenship in Israel is obtained (cp. John x. 1 ff.). It is therefore quite natural that St Matthew applies to him the word of the prophet Hosea, originally spoken of the people Israel, "Out of Egypt have I called my son" (ii. 15, xi. 1).

Christ is also the son of David, and as such He re-establishes the unity between Israel and Judah proclaimed in the prophetic promises of the Old Testament. Perhaps it is not unimportant from a theological point of view that He, being Himself of the tribe of Judah and born in Bethlehem, grew up in Galilee and there recruited most of His followers and intimate friends. His interest in the Samaritans must

35

certainly be regarded from this point of view; He gathers
His scattered people in a new higher unity, the Church.

He is a king, but throughout His ministry He rejects
every political interpretation of His Messianic vocation, the
external warfare of the Kingdom of God having come to an
end. His kingdom is not of this world (John xviii. 36);
He is the Suffering Servant giving His life as a ransom for
many and thereby inaugurating the New Covenant. The
prophecies about the empire of Israel thus get a new interpretation in His Person; He has all power in heaven and
earth and sends out His disciples to win the whole world by
making disciples of all nations (Matt. xxviii. 18–19). This
does not imply tyranny and oppression, but, on the contrary,
that the ancient enmity between Israel and the other nations
is ended by the destruction of the barrier, so that even
goyim obtain citizenship in Israel (Eph. ii. 11–12). In this
way Yahweh's war in the Old Testament is brought to final
victory, in a peace giving equal rights to all nations.

But the connection with the people of the old covenant
remains; it is the seed, the root of God's new people.
Salvation means that all nations become partakers of the
promises at first given only to Israel. Israel is the stem into
which the nations are grafted (Rom. xi. 1 ff.), and if our
interpretation of the Root and Stem of Jesse, of the Branch
and the Servant, as the Remnant *par excellence* is right, then
Christ is Himself *the* Remnant, He is the Holy Seed, in
Himself representing the whole of Israel. The way to
renewal for Him, as for Israel in the Old Testament, and for
His followers in the Church, leads through death to life.

I have done no more than to make a few suggestions about
Christ as the beginning and Creator of the new People of
God, gathering together and recapitulating in Himself all the
conceptions of God's people in the Old Testament, which
receive their organic unity in Him.

III

JESUS, ST JOHN AND ST PAUL

Anton Fridrichsen

I

DISCUSSIONS OF THE PROBLEM of Jesus and St Paul for a long time assumed a form which was inappropriate and therefore unproductive. The two figures were compared as religious personalities; the relation between their "religions" was canvassed. Had they the same religion? "Jesus" in those days meant the Sermon on the Mount and the parables, as they were then interpreted, *i.e.* as a purified, reformed and spiritualized Judaism—a renewal and perfection of the ethical monotheism of the great prophets of Israel. When Jesus, thus conceived of, was compared with St Paul, the most favourable conclusion possible was that St Paul, in spite of everything, had a good deal in common with Jesus; he had really understood something of the gospel of Jesus, and above all had laid hold on *Love*—the love of God, the love of Jesus, the commandment to love. But it had to be admitted that this simple central theme was obscured, and in various ways paralysed by dogma, by myth and by gnosis. Evidently St Paul was of a different religious type from Jesus; he was a theologian and mystic who lived in his spiritual experiences, so that he lacked any real sense for or interest in the historical person of Jesus, and did not want to have any real contact with it. The words of Jesus were of no importance to him. He did not build on them, but formed his own message and doctrine, and they were on quite different lines, both as to ideas and as to terms.

This whole argument makes a twofold mistake. It overlooks or denies the Messianic aspect of the person and work of Jesus and, proceeding to comparisons, it parallels Jesus the Messiah in *His* historical situation with the Messiah's Apostle in *his*. Two incomparable things are thus contrasted. But Jesus and St Paul ought to be confronted, not as religious types or as personalities, but *in their historical relation to each other*. What is the nature of this relation?

It is not as though St Paul were a disciple who, having been moulded in the school of Jesus, handed down the tradition of His teaching and commented on it. On the contrary, St Paul was an *Apostle* who preached the death and resurrection of the Messiah, and stated the meaning and consequences of events which were invested with the significance of a new æon. If he were a disciple, a hander on of tradition and a commentator, the critical question whether his "religion" agreed with that of Jesus would be legitimate. It would then also be of interest to draw a comparison between Jesus's psychological make-up and his, setting the two religious personalities face to face. But as St Paul is the Apostle of Jesus Christ proclaiming the eschatological message of the crucified Messiah and the reality of the Resurrection, the critical question must be quite different. The problem that is relevant, scientific and theological is whether by his gospel and his teaching St Paul fulfilled the intention of Jesus, or whether he distorted it, abandoning the foundation on which Jesus stood, acted, spoke, suffered and died. Everything depends upon the result of this inquiry.

If in his message and teaching the Apostle Paul aimed at fulfilling the intention of Jesus, then it is quite natural that he should speak another language than Jesus Himself, who proclaimed in a Jewish environment that the Kingdom of God was at hand. In St Paul's situation and with his commission it was natural and necessary for him to build not upon the historical message of Jesus, but upon the fact of the cross and the resurrection, his function being to develop the significance of this fact. In this connection, the study of St Paul's "religious personality", of his "religion", is only of interest in so far as it facilitates our understanding of his writings, his style and his thought. To draw a comparison between Jesus and St Paul as religious personalities, preachers and teachers may not be out of place if one wishes to set up a gallery of "great religious personalities", a panorama without any theological interest, but capable of diverting and edifying people who, like Alexander Severus, are occupied in setting up a syncretistic pantheon in the sanctuary of their homes. If we isolate great religious personalities from their historical environment and mutual relationship, placing them beside each other on the same level, our findings may at best be of some interest to a commonplace religious phenomenology which deals with general categories; they can be of no assistance to the understanding of a concrete historical situation like the one with which we are here concerned.

Jesus's teaching, His Sermon on the Mount, and His parables belong to His activity among God's people of old times, in the last days of the ancient era. Formally and objectively they bear the stamp of that activity, and of its special purpose in preparing the congregation of the Jewish Synagogue for the Kingdom of God. Thus they belong to the old age. But, at the same time, they bear the new one within them. Therefore it has been possible for them to be adopted by the Church, and in the light of the Resurrection, and the fellowship of the Spirit, to become the Word of the Lord to His redeemed people. St Paul knew them in this sense, and no doubt he utilized them in the instruction of his congregations. But he was not confined to them in his interpretation of the reality of the resurrection. Here his object was, of course, to explain to Jews and Greeks the meaning of the Messiah's death and of His resurrection on the third day according to the Scriptures.

As has been already pointed out, St Paul was not a disciple of Jesus in the sense of handing down His tradition and interpreting His teaching. But furthermore, *Jesus never had a disciple of this kind at all.* This is a particularly important and remarkable fact, and more than anything else it goes to prove that Jesus did not proclaim a religious wisdom, a doctrine of life and how to live it, but an urgent message about what is now taking place and what is required of us. Matthew and Luke have preserved the Sermon on the Mount and the parables, not as a doctrine to be accepted and interpreted, but as an expression of the will and being of our Heavenly Lord. The word, the commandment, the metaphor must not be separated from Jesus's own Person as the Saviour perfected and glorified through death. They possess their truth and authenticity only in His Church, which is united to Him through faith, the Spirit, and the sacraments. There is no fundamental difference between the attitude of St Matthew or St Luke to the words of Jesus and that of St Paul. The Evangelists, the recorders and preservers of the Word of God, witness in harmony with St Paul that Jesus, the Son of Man, claimed to be the Messiah, the King in the Kingdom of God, the First-Born of the new generation, the Saviour of redeemed Israel. St Paul carried out the intention of Jesus when he proclaimed Jesus Christ crucified and risen, and explained both to the Jews and to the Gentiles what this meant and what was consequently required of them.

Anyone following the slogan "Back to Jesus!" will therefore go further back than he intends. He will go past Jesus and land in the Synagogue. He will simply take his stand on the Sermon on the Mount and the parables, believing himself to be in the footsteps of Jesus. But even when preaching the Sermon on the Mount and relating His parables, Jesus is on His way to Calvary and the glory of the Father. The Messiah on the Mount was the Son of Man. If we do not realize this, we are stuck in an *interpretatio Judaica* of His words. The form of these words is conditioned by the situation: the Kingdom of God is at hand! But in spirit they point forward: The Lord is risen! And only in the light of the Resurrection is their full meaning revealed. It is only through communion with our Lord in His death and Resurrection that the precepts of the Sermon on the Mount become a law of life actually in force, and the secret of the parables is revealed.

The caption "in Christ" (*en Christō*) may be placed above everything that St Paul says. That is the formula of the new age which is to last until "in Christ" is superseded by "with Christ" (*syn Christō*). He who believes the Gospel of the crucified and risen Jesus is in Christ and a new creation, adopted into the Body which was inaugurated by the Lord's resurrection from the dead and which lives in Him. This truth has its external expression in the fact that the believer is incorporated into the Church through baptism, and into the life of sacramental unity with the Church. Being "in Christ", being rooted in the faith, means being inseparably bound to the Ecclesia and its services, ministrations and regulations. St Paul neither knows nor recognizes any "spiritual" religion which can be probably cultivated by the individual in experience and thought; the Church is both the sphere and the centre of all Christian life. To be "in Christ" is more than an idea or an ideal; it is a visible and tangible reality, through which the whole invisible being of Christ is communicated to the believer.

It became the task of St Paul in the history of the Church to found and establish this understanding of what Christianity is, as the state of being in Christ. He realized and exemplified the formula in his personal life; but, as we are primarily concerned with the historical problems of Primitive Christianity, we must especially direct our attention to St Paul's contribution to our understanding of it. He established an interpretation of Christianity and gave it classical expression, and did all this in connection with a mission which founded the Church in the principal countries of the civilized world. In view of the Apostle's contribution, we are faced by a twofold question: Did St Paul fulfil the intention of Jesus? And secondly, Where does he stand in the history of thought with his formula "in Christ"?

The first question can be answered without more ado in the affirmative, now that the tradition of the Gospels regarding Jesus's designation of Himself and His self-consciousness has passed intact through the fires of criticism. The realization of the significance of Jesus's self-awarded title "Son of Man" for His Messianic activity has had decisive consequences for the problem of Jesus and St Paul. In particular, the fact that the conception of the Church is already met with in the thought, words and activity of Jesus provides us with a firm stepping-stone from Him to St Paul, the founder of churches. It is not true that the Pauline "in Christ" is absolutely new, originating in the personal experience of the Apostle. Rather, the believer's relation to Christ, as St Paul understands it, is the fulfilment of Jesus's teaching about discipleship, made possible by the resurrection, and expressed in terms of it; though St Paul's teaching naturally bears the stamp of his own religious individuality. The relation between the Pauline idea of the Church and the belief of the Son of Man regarding the Israel He had come to redeem, sanctify and renew by the sacrifice of His life is, in fact, clear and unmistakable.

The *Eucharist* deserves special attention in this connection, since, with the exception of the cross, it is almost the only historical reference in St Paul's letters to the earthly life of the Lord. Probably no one now seriously believes that the narratives of the Lord's Supper in the Synoptic Gospels are merely an antedating of the Eucharistic ritual of the later Church. In the Gospel of St Mark we have a largely reliable, though of course an extremely condensed, account of what took place on that occasion; and there should be no doubt that, by what He did and said, Jesus wished to provide for continued communion between Himself and His disciples after His departure. He associated His presence with the breaking of the bread by saying "This is my body", *i.e.* this is myself. Moreover, He declared that a new covenant would be established by His sacrificial death, and that whoever drinks of the cup will be received into, or renewed in, the covenant. This is also St Paul's teaching regarding the Eucharist in i Corinthians xi. The agreement between the Messiah and His Apostle is cardinal. Jesus made the provision that the communion between Himself and His disciples at the Last Supper should thereafter be the pattern for sacramental communion between them. In the Pauline form of the words of institution Jesus says, "This do ye . . . in remembrance of me." History and cult are joined in a unity in the Holy Communion. The "anamnesis" also includes the cultic presence. An eschatological aspect belongs to it. Jesus said, "I will drink no more of the fruit of the vine until that day that I drink it new in the kingdom of God." St Paul writes, "As often as ye eat this bread, and drink this cup, ye do show the Lord's death till he come."

The Lord and His Apostle stand on the same foundation. This is also evident from the fact that for St Paul the decisive and fundamental word is *faith*. "From faith to faith." Faith builds upon history and includes it, but associates it with the present, and aspires to the future consummation. Faith is faith in the Gospel with its historical facts; but at the same time it is faith in the living, ever present and coming Lord. To St Paul, past and present facts converge in one eschatological reality. In the consciousness of faith, as well as in sacramental observance, there cannot be one without the other.

It is obvious, however, that St Paul did not consider it to be his duty expressly to emphasize this connection, and to underline or give prominence to the foundation of faith in history. To him the connection with history is already present in the very concept of faith itself, and to him a more urgent matter is to elucidate the meaning of faith as a basis of justification in the New Covenant. *Justification by faith* is the fundamental theme of St Paul's message and teaching. Realizing this, we are confronted with the other question, the position of St Paul in the history of thought, or rather in the history of theology and of the Primitive Church.

It fell to St Paul to interpret the *righteousness* of the New Covenant to the Church. For this he possessed special qualifications. The situation confronting him when he was called to become the "Apostle to the Gentiles" also demanded an authoritative interpretation of the reality of Christ from the point of view of righteousness. The Law and the works of the Law were the foundation of righteousness in Israel, in Palestinian Judaism as well as in Hellenistic;

43

the question arose what position the Law was to have in the new Israel, among the redeemed and sanctified eschatological people of God.

It is from the very outset a question of *righteousness*, of the revealed will of God and of His approval. St Paul had no inclination towards any other type of religion. On his missionary journeys, among all the Jews, and also among many of the Greeks, he met the question: How shall I become righteous, attain the standard, fulfil the supreme demand of the Deity, stand before the judgement? This was the traditional line of religious inquiry among the Jews, the only thing that mattered, the central question of life and death. But the Greeks often had a tendency in the same direction. The mystery element in popular Greek religion is generally exaggerated. The Stoa, and the impulses emerging from it, were the strongest spiritual forces in the Hellenistic world. And in its practical popular form the Stoa exhibited a pronounced moralism with deep roots in the Hellenistic conception of life, in the philosophy of the people with its rigorously ethical principle of retaliation, a Greek legalism with unwritten though absolutely binding laws. Sin, guilt, judgement, punishment, forgiveness—all these were concepts no less vital and crucial among Greeks than among Jews. The guilt of the past and the approaching day of reckoning and retribution were urgent practical problems occupying and dominating men's minds. When the subject of salvation was mentioned, there were many among the Greeks also whose conscience and sense of guilt were stirred.

The Gospel preached by St Paul was therefore a "power unto salvation" both to the Jew and to the Greek. And this Gospel had its centre in *justification*. One of the greatest mistakes of Albert Schweitzer has been to consider the doctrine of justification as a polemical by-product of Pauline thought, a theoretical auxiliary without practical significance. On the contrary, a proper understanding of St Paul must proceed from his teaching about how man is justified by faith in God's act of justification. St Paul's language is itself

44

significant; the question is not how man by his own activity gains the approval of God, but how, by being adopted into living fellowship with Christ, he becomes the child of God, receives Christ's own righteousness and becomes a partaker of His life and being. This message was preached by St Paul to Jews and Gentiles, and he laboured unceasingly to elucidate the implications and consequences of it, and to found his doctrine on Scripture. In this way he interpreted the situation created by the saving work of the Messiah and the meaning of the New Covenant and its demand for faith.

How far, it may be asked, did the Apostle fulfil the intentions of Jesus in this respect?

With regard to the question of righteousness, the antithesis so radically formulated in St Paul between the works of the law and faith is clearly not found in the teaching of Jesus. Nevertheless we venture to assert that St Paul's teaching about man's justification by faith in Christ has its root and basis in the message and life of Jesus, and in principle expresses His will and intention. We must develop this line of thought more fully.

"Repent ye and believe the gospel" was the message of Jesus to the people of Israel when the fullness of time was come. This message found a hearing among the simple-minded, the humble and the poor, whereas the truth was hidden from the wise and prudent. Evidently we find ourselves in quite a different atmosphere to that of Jewish legalism; here other standards are in force, for the very reason that the fullness of time has come. The Messiah and the Kingdom are at hand; God is now acting decisively and conclusively; His invitation is extended through the Son of Man. Man must enter through faith and obedience into what is now taking place, accept the invitation, and consequently abandon his own way, unreservedly handing himself over to the divine initiative and receiving the Kingdom. Fundamentally this is the same eschatological revolution of Judaism as St Paul taught in his doctrine of justification; God creates the possibility of salvation, not by promulgating a number of new commandments and prohibitions to be

45

observed, but by establishing the "Kingdom" (Jesus), a "Righteousness" (St Paul) in which He receives willing and responsive men, accepting them into His love and royal grace. This love and grace are now the principle of life, the power and the rule of those who have been made righteous.

The radical and revolutionary elements of this are clear from St Paul's terminology: the sinner is justified freely by grace. It sounds paradoxical, and it is deliberately so. But in order to understand St Paul correctly, we must always remember that the statement, God justifies the sinner by grace without any merit on the part of man, is not a mere religious truism, but an eschatological statement. It interprets the meaning of the situation created by the coming of the Messiah. It was not in force earlier, although it was in God's thought, intention and plan from the beginning. It is for *the present* that this message is intended, and, as it is being proclaimed, the possibility of justification is opened to the hearers. The Gospel proclaims what has become a reality in the time of fulfilment, when God's dealings with Israel attain their goal and are fulfilled. Thus the paradox of St Paul's teaching does not consist in an inversion of the view hitherto current in consequence of a reformer's deeper insight; it expresses a totally and radically changed situation.

If this is the case, it is of fundamental importance to our purpose to find out whether the logia and activity of Jesus possessed this eschatological character. What is paradoxical and revolutionary in Jesus's teaching and way of life is frequently expressed in the gospel tradition, *e.g.* in the parable of the labourers in the vineyard, in that of the Pharisee and the Publican, and in those concerning the nature of the Kingdom of God, as well as in His dealings with publicans and sinners. But when He upsets all conventional Jewish ideas, He does not do so in order to correct Judaism, but as a revelation of what is now, in the Messianic age, in force as law and as the norm of the relation between God and His people. The sin of the Pharisees and the

46

Scribes is not that they have maintained false doctrine, but that they do not believe in Him who is sent by the Father. On this vital point we find fundamental agreement between Jesus and St Paul, whatever difference there may be in their presentation of it.   Both for the Lord and for His Apostle it is ultimately a question of faith in and obedience to the eschatological message.

"Believe the Gospel" is the primary message of both Jesus and St Paul.   There has been no lack of attempts to trace Pauline influence in the synopsis of the sermon by Jesus given by St Mark in the beginning of his Gospel.   But this summary agrees so well with what Jesus says in other places regarding the nature of the Kingdom and receptiveness for the Word that we have no reason to question the authenticity of the teaching of Jesus as recorded or formulated by St Mark. In this connection we may especially remind ourselves of the Parable of the Sower (Mark iv).   The theme of this parable is an eschatological message concerning faith.   Only when the seed falls on good ground, where the Word finds genuine faith, does it bear fruit.

It is impossible to indicate any fundamental and essential difference between Jesus and St Paul.   The apparent discrepancy depends on the difference of the situations before and after Easter and Pentecost.   The Easter gospel, with its religious and ethical consequences, is latent in the message of Jesus concerning the Kingdom of God and in His presentation of Himself as the Son of Man.

Such a statement may seem bold in view of the fact that, after Easter and Pentecost, faith and life in the Church are wholly determined by the cross and the resurrection, by baptism and the Holy Spirit, themes which were naturally lacking in the teaching of Jesus Himself, as it appears in synoptic tradition.   In view of this fact, must not the old distinction between the gospel taught by Jesus and the gospel concerning Jesus Christ be maintained after all? Is there any presentation of Biblical theology capable of bridging these two views?   Are we not finally obliged to make the choice between the Sermon on the Mount and the

Lord's Prayer on the one hand, and Pauline (and Johannine) dogmatics on the other?

We are warned not to draw a hasty and positive conclusion of this kind by the fact that "the second Gospel" demonstrably originated directly from "the first". This bears testimony to the fact that the predisposition to believe in Easter and the experience of Pentecost arose out of the person of Jesus and His work. The Sermon on the Mount and the Lord's Prayer are not Jewish documents; they do not represent a sublimated and profounder Judaism. They are expressions of religious reality in the time of fulfilment, in the presence of the Son of Man. They epitomize and anticipate what is subsequently fully revealed and made central to the life of the Church. Consequently, Easter and Pentecost did not imply that the tradition from Galilee and Jerusalem regarding Jesus became obsolete and was forgotten. On the contrary, even the earliest Christians found edification and guidance in the story of Jesus. Then as to-day, the Church's possession of her risen Lord and His Spirit was set before the congregation in the gospel lections of public worship which present the Saviour in His incarnate and historical life. It is on this picture that faith is founded. It is essential that faith should see the glorified Lord and Jesus in the flesh as one and the same. Then the difference between the gospel portrait of Jesus and the "dogmas" of belief in Easter is not a hindrance or a burden but something natural, self-evident and necessary. There is one and the same person and activity, at different stages of one and the same continuous course of events, the course of God's dealings with Israel and the world in the last times through His Son, in the fullness of time when the eschatological people of God, the people of faith, are established in the presence of the Son of Man and incorporated as His body in the world.

The problem of "Jesus and St Paul" must be solved in this way and from this point of view. St Paul is the interpreter of the significance of the eschatological situation after the resurrection from the aspect of righteousness. He thereby fulfils the intention of the message of Jesus concerning

48

the Kingdom of God, and gives faithful expression to what was already implicit in the message of Jesus: "Repent ye and believe the gospel!"

II

St John and *St Paul* are on the same level as interpreters of the reality of the Resurrection in the Primitive Church. It was long customary to discuss the history of the development of Primitive Christianity according to the scheme: Jesus (the Synoptics)—St Paul—St John. St John represents the climax of the Hellenization of Christianity; he stands on the shoulders of St Paul and continues his work in that he Hellenizes the historical portrait of Jesus also. This was of little significance to St Paul, who was content to dogmatize the Risen Lord; St John dogmatizes the man Jesus even before His resurrection, thus bringing about the radical Hellenization of the Gospel.

This scheme of development has had to be abandoned. St John is independent of St Paul. On the other hand, he is dependent on a tradition which has its roots in Jerusalem and ultimately in the immediate circle of Jesus. It is on this tradition and on its interpretation and formulation in the Ephesian Church that he founded his gospel. Thus, St John does not stand on the shoulders of St Paul, but he is on a par with him as an independent interpreter of Christ in the Church. His interpretation strikes off into other paths than that of St Paul. The difference concerns both form and theological structure, and it is easy to see how its form and matter are related. St Paul discusses the concept of righteousness under the New Covenant, in an epistle or treatise. St John found himself confronted by another task, to bind the contents of Christian faith and the religious experience of the Church inseparably together with the historical foundation of faith, in the person and works of Jesus in the flesh. His interest is anti-Gnostic, and his main purpose is to show the unity between the risen, glorified Lord

D 49

and the Word that was made flesh, the Jesus of Galilee and Jerusalem. For this purpose a gospel was the natural and suitable form. Accordingly, St John presents an interpretation of Jesus which shows how the faith and religious experience of the Church are inherent in the words and activity of Jesus in His capacity as the Messiah of Israel. This is St John's way of interpreting the reality of the Resurrection. Objectively viewed, what is the relation of this interpretation to that of St Paul?

No words need be wasted regarding the difference; it is sufficiently obvious. Nor is it of decisive importance to be able to show specific similarities. The question is whether a fundamental agreement can be pointed out between the two primitive theologians of the Church, testifying to a common basic origin of their teaching.

The key-words of St Paul are *faith* and *righteousness*; those of St John *faith* and (*eternal*) *life*. In both there is the eschatological reality of Christ, created through the works of Jesus, His death and Resurrection, and actualized through the Gospel, the Word in the Church, within the sacramental communion of the Church in her unity with the Risen Lord. Here we have the fundamental point of agreement between St Paul and St John; and we can ascertain that "life" according to St John and "righteousness" according to St Paul are two expressions for the same thing, only with a different emphasis. In both cases there is communion of fallen and lost man with his Creator—a communion which is freely bestowed through faith in Jesus Christ, the Son. It is a fellowship which man receives and possesses through personal and living communion with the Son. Its antithesis is the same in both St Paul and St John: unbelief, condemnation and death; and it is eschatological, gaining its validity entirely from the story of Christ.

"Righteousness" and "life" are identical ideas and realities in the Old Testament. The righteous man, who lives wholeheartedly in the Covenant, possesses life in union with God and His people; his entire being is infused with peace and blessing. There is no priority; righteousness is life, and life is righteousness. A sharper differentiation between the concepts was made in Judaism because righteousness was tied to the commandments, and, in the resurrection, life was the reward for a righteousness acquired through obedience to the Law. But in the Church, the eschatological people of God, we find that the organic relation between righteousness and life is established on a new foundation. Now they are one "in Christ". St Paul's extensive use of legal arguments in his polemics against Jews and Judaizers, who try to gain righteousness and life apart from Christ, must not conceal the fact that, in his opinion, righteousness is rooted in the Covenant itself, the new Covenant, the reality of faith created by God through Christ and actualized through the Gospel. For St Paul, to be righteous is to abide with one's whole being in this Covenant, to be "in Christ". And as the righteousness of God consists in His creating the reality of Christ, so the righteousness which the believer receives in Christ is God's own righteousness and life received in and through Christ.

As a matter of fact, the Pauline and the Johannine lines of thought converge. The divergence in form, terminology and structure depends upon the different characters and historical positions of the interpreters. St Paul, the former Pharisee, was settling accounts with Judaism; St John, rooted in the tradition of Jesus, was building up a defence against a "spiritual" gnosis. St John's purpose is indicated in the words by which the Evangelist ends his Gospel (xx. 31): "These (signs) are written, that ye might believe that Jesus is the Messiah, the Son of God; and that believing ye might have life through His name." Faith is faith in Jesus as the Son of God and the Word who became flesh. Faith is a belief that He who was Man among men was sent by God to be the Saviour. The historical person, Jesus of Nazareth in Galilee, is the foundation and the object of faith. To bear testimony to Him constitutes faith (xvii. 20 ff.). It is obvious that St John betrays a different emphasis than St Paul. Still, there is no real divergence between them, as both of them remain within one and the same indivisible eschatological reality, connected with Jesus, His life, death and resurrection. Within this single scheme St Paul and St John lay stress on different elements, but all the time both proceed from the whole and take it into account. Furthermore, it is significant that in St John too "the Jews" represent unbelief; they refuse to acknowledge Jesus as sent by God, to recognize Him as the herald of definite eschatological events and to subordinate themselves to them. In essence this is the same as when St Paul accuses the Jews because they will not abandon their own righteousness and receive God's righteousness in Christ (Rom. x. 3).

Finally, it must be pointed out that both St Paul and St John present Jesus as the pattern according to which man is to be fashioned in the new people of God. It is not a question of a mechanical *imitatio*, but of obedience to His will and example, in the communion with Him of faith and love, and with His image before our eyes. This image is not to be copied; it is to operate in conjunction with the new commandment, and, through the work of the Spirit in him and in the Church, the man who is faithful and obedient is to become the follower of Jesus. "If any man serve me, let him follow me" (John xii. 26). "If ye continue in my word, then are ye my disciples indeed" (John viii. 31). "The word of Jesus" is His historical revelation. God "predestined us to be conformed to the image of His Son" . . . "changed into the same image" . . . "that He might be the firstborn among many brethren" (Rom. viii. 29. Cp. 2 Cor. iii. 18). Neither St John nor St Paul would have been able to write such words unless the historical portrait of Jesus, as it appears in His words, His deeds and His sufferings, were the living background and primary foundation of all their religious ideas and doctrines.

III

We have no definite information about St Paul's picture of Jesus in the flesh. On the other hand, we possess a Johannine portrait of Him; and this being so, we must examine its relation to the picture drawn by the Synoptists. We are then confronted by the problem of *St John and the Synoptists*, which is one of the most important problems for modern Biblical research. Ever since it was raised in the 1770's it has continually exercised the minds of New Testament scholars. The Johannine controversy is still going on; and, as yet, it has had no definite solution. However, it has not been in vain. Even if the Fourth Gospel still raises great problems which will perhaps remain unsolved, it can nevertheless be claimed that a view of the Fourth Gospel is being crystallized which is at once "critical" and positive. It is not now possible to rehearse and elaborate this view in detail; it can only be briefly and summarily alluded to.

To an older generation it seemed self-evident that the Gospel of St John must be regarded as altogether secondary to the Synoptic Gospels. The life and teaching of Jesus are to be found in the Gospel of St Mark and in the logia-source of St Matthew and St Luke. In St John we do not find history, but a theological construction on the basis of, and with its starting-point in, certain Synoptic motifs. The Evangelist aimed at describing the work and teaching of Jesus, His death and Resurrection, in forms and language which appealed to his own religious outlook and experience. Consequently Jesus speaks St John's own language and proclaims his thoughts. The narratives are saturated with Johannine Christ-mysticism and Johannine speculation; they have a double basis, since a symbolic and allegorical character has been added to them which has nothing to do with authentic history. Everywhere the theological reflections of the Evangelist, or of the Johannine circle, obtrude themselves; and when in certain indirect allusions he pretends that the Gospel was written by one of Jesus's disciples and most intimate friends, this is a literary artifice to confer the highest rank and authority on the book. Thus the Gospel of St John does not belong to history except as a factor in, and an original document for, the history of dogma. The Evangelist, or his circle, has developed Pauline theology further towards mysticism, has purified its language from all Judaism, and subordinated it to the universal scope of the Greek notion of the Logos.

This critical view of St John's Gospel is based on patent facts. But have the right conclusions been drawn from them?

It is certainly beyond dispute that the Synoptic Gospels present the strictly "historical" picture of Jesus in the sense that the parables, the Sermon on the Mount, and specific details of the historical setting present us with history as it was immediately manifested by Jesus Himself in His words and deeds. Thus it came to pass, thus He spoke and acted. There can be no doubt that the presentation of St John is strongly and radically stylized. But does this imply that the Fourth Gospel is not "historical"?

In our days this question has begun to challenge Johannine research. It is extremely interesting to observe developments in this field. We have witnessed a change of views affecting more problems than the Johannine. It embraces our attitude towards, and our estimate of, the *entire* tradition regarding Jesus, all Biblical tradition and indeed all ancient religious tradition in general. The problem is difficult to state in a few sentences; but it is connected with what was alluded to in the beginning of this essay, the break with the so-called "Historico-critical School" of the nineteenth century. Characteristic positions of that School are, as already pointed out, evolutionism, idealism and, connected with these two "isms", relativism. In its eyes the purpose of criticizing an ancient historical text is, above all, to find the "authentic" material, the reliable biographical data which provide evidence for the life, character and views of the persons under discussion. Furthermore, it is necessary to examine their environment and the creative and formative elements operative in it. What is individual and personal is largely determined in its development by underlying dynamic and conflicting trends. The purpose of historical research is to present what is individual and personal in strict relation to them, because they are ultimately decisive. The application of this method in research concerning Jesus led inevitably to preposterous results. A picture of Jesus was drawn which was simply the idealized self-portrait of man in the nineteenth century. When this portrait is studied, St Paul and St John inevitably stand out as founders of a new religion quite different from that taught by Jesus. In the Synoptic material as shaped by tradition there was discovered an historical kernel consisting of certain facts and words of Jesus; all the rest was secondary material, the product of the theologizing of the Church.

Gradually, however, the conviction has grown that this is not the way to study and interpret ancient Eastern religious documents. An Israelite prophet or a Jewish Messiah cannot be understood solely in terms of Western thought in the nineteenth century. The man of God is never isolated. He is always the centre of a circle taught by his words and example, in which his manner of life and teaching continues after his death. What is taught and written in this circle is ultimately derived from its founder and embodies his life and character. When we, the children of a later age and of another culture, wish to understand such a person and his period, we must return to tradition and inquire there; but our inquiry must be made with due understanding of local peculiarities. Only with such a sympathetic understanding is it possible to estimate a tradition as a source of history. No appreciation can be acquired without insight into the habits of life and thought of prophetic circles in ancient Israel, or of Jews of Rabbinic education and Messianic outlook. It will become clear that tradition is an excellent source for history, if the history we have in mind is the conduct of life in associations governed and influenced by persons who in some extraordinary way speak with divine authority. But it will soon also be found that no biographical or psychological account of such figures can be given. They cannot be viewed as individualists in their consciousness or their behaviour; their souls are of quite a different structure from those of modern European men. Real understanding is only possible after considering the legacy they leave to their circles, and the tradition formed, preserved and continually propagated within them. This of course does not imply that in principle one is to refrain from isolating earlier and later strata within a tradition, or from determining as far as possible, by critical observation and reflection, facts and utterances immediately associated with whatever person is the object of research. But it means that one cannot hope in this way to study the character of a prophet as a modern historian would. No conception of him can be formed except by observing how he was remembered, described and quoted, and what was handed down about him. All these things form a totality of which he was the soul, because he did not keep his soul to himself, but gave himself to those who received his words, his nature and his will into themselves. Therefore, from the point of view of what is demanded in a modern biography, any statement concerning men of God in the ancient East must appear extremely unsatisfactory, uncertain and fragmentary as an exercise in biography or in character study. But to one who has liberated himself from the narrow view and limited experience of the Historico-critical School, tradition itself in all its abundance, variation and multiplicity will be the mirror in which historical reality is reflected. What has here been stated in general terms is relevant to a long line of Biblical persons, to Isaiah and Jeremiah as well as to Jesus and John the Baptist.

If we adopt this point of view, the following question regarding the Fourth Gospel will then arise: Does the Gospel of St John contain authentic tradition, or is it pseudo-tradition, a result of the intentional fabrication of history? To put the question is to answer it. What is stated in the Fourth Gospel possesses its own independent historical value in relation to the Synoptic Gospels; on this question there is now virtual unanimity among scholars. And there is no reason to doubt that the Johannine logia tradition originated and received its form in Jesus's own circle of disciples. It has its origin in the circle of the Master under the inspiration of His Person and teaching.

If St Peter has left his stamp on the Synoptic tradition,

as in all appearance he has, then St John, the disciple of Jesus—whether it was the Apostle or the Presbyter is of no real importance—set the tone of the Fourth Gospel. The literary work which we find in the New Testament is of course the final result of several decades. The tradition has had a history in which both oral narrative or teaching and written records have played their part as stages in its development. But the history of the various materials which now comprise the Gospel of St John cannot be reconstructed by us. All attempts constitute mere arbitrary hypotheses. We can only establish the fact that there are unmistakable traces of a collection of materials and of redaction. What can be asserted is that the final literary form is faithful to the teaching of its sources, and through them to that of Jesus Himself. The Evangelist himself was soaked in his material, and consequently he faithfully transmits both its form and its substance.

Thus the Gospel of St John, full as it is of the ideas and language of the Beloved Disciple and of his circle, is an authentic historical testimony to Jesus. The Evangelist endeavours to present a portrait of Jesus like that which he had received and adopted from the first eye-witnesses and which survived in the Church to which he belonged.

Confronted with the problem of "St John and the Synoptics", we do not think it valid to brand the Gospel of St John as an historically inferior product of the mysticism and speculation of a later age. The Synoptists and St John alike present us with a portrait of Jesus which is ultimately derived from personal observation, experience and impression. It is the same Person and the same historical truth which is communicated in both these branches of tradition. They are of equal value as sources for our knowledge of Jesus, His teaching and mission. They complete each other. St John presents a profounder interpretation of the portrait of Jesus presented by the Synoptists. They are dominated by the Messianic idea and the image of the Son of Man. St John goes deeper: the profounder purposes of Jesus in His preaching and activity as Messiah and Son of Man are

57

revealed in the Johannine portrait of the Son who was sent by the Father to accomplish His work in the world. From this point of view it stands to reason that our historical use of St John will not be simply to fuse the Fourth Gospel with the Synoptics. The two portraits of Jesus must stand independently. *But they must be viewed together*. Then we shall see one consistent historical reality.

We may illustrate this by a review of two great landmarks of Christological controversy during the last hundred years, the work of Baur and of Schweitzer, before drawing some conclusions about future study of the person of Jesus Christ.

Ferd. Chr. Baur found the solution of the historical problem of Primitive Christianity in a dialectical movement through antitheses to the higher unity of the Catholic Church. The theology of the turn of the century with its evolutionist view of history, its psychological method of interpretation and its personal idealism, regarded the primitive history of Christianity as a rapid Hellenization of the Gospel, in which, however, the majestic ethical and religious personality of Jesus continued to assert its influence in the tranquil and inmost sanctuary of the Christian soul. What has subsequent Biblical scholarship put in its place? Its substitute is the *eschatological* view of history, which relates *Jesus Christ and His Church* in one organic and indissoluble unity.

It was the genius of Albert Schweitzer that gave the death-blow to the liberal historical view when he pointed out that both Jesus and St Paul take their stand on the same dogmatic foundation, that of Messianism. An organic connection between Christ and His Apostle is then disclosed. St Paul teaches the consequences of the life of Jesus, and interprets it with apostolic authority. Schweitzer, to be sure, is guilty of distortions. He makes Jesus a desperate apocalyptic fanatic who by His self-provoked death strove to force the immediate coming of the Kingdom of God. According to Schweitzer's presentation, St Paul is an eschatological mystic for whom the life and teaching of Jesus were of no significance; the only matter of importance to him was the sacramental supra-mundane life communicated to believers by Christ after the resurrection. St John is a sheer mystic, having lost every connection with the historical Jesus. His Gospel is a myth, which provides the contents and character of the Christian mystery. In his new teaching St Paul still stands entirely on the foundation of Judaism; St John is a Hellenist throughout. These misinterpretations, however, are of slight significance in contrast to the fundamental contribution Schweitzer made, which overthrew modern constructions and restored New Testament research to the *terra firma* of Biblical reality. He was not the first to realize and insist upon the eschatological outlook of the New Testament. But he was the first to discern the tremendous consequences of eschatological interpretation for Biblical scholarship as well as for all theology. Hence he must be placed beside Baur in the history of theology as a pioneer of research into the historical problems of Primitive Christianity.

This study is still in its infancy, even if it already has an extensive and rich history. It has been going on for more than a hundred years; Baur sketched his view for the first time in a small publication in 1831. But the history of the interpretation of the Bible is in many ways so intimately connected with the development and transformation of the entire spiritual situation that the new views need a long time to mature, grow clearer, and establish their effects in every direction. We are witnessing the commencement of a new era in Biblical scholarship with important consequences for the attitude of the Church towards the Bible and for its use of it. Both in practical religion and in theology we are living in a transitional epoch with all its confusion and obscurity, but also with the encouragements and hopes afforded by these new impulses. What then is the objective of action on the Biblical front?

It is the discovery of the fundamental unity of the Bible. But this unity is not a uniformity. On the contrary, it is to the interest of faith to have disclosed variety, growth and movement along the Biblical images; for our aim is to discern history, the continuity of events, reality working and being transformed—in short, eschatological fulfilment in preparation under the old Israel, in realization through Jesus Christ, and in interpretation by His Church. The whole New Testament falls within this syllabus, and all its books can be arranged within it and be seen to blend into a complete unity.

With such an outlook, one is bound to adopt a different view regarding the historical problems of Primitive Christianity from that of liberal theology. In so doing there is no question of departing from or denying the principles governing all modern scientific historical research, such as those of literary criticism, the history of religion and culture, and psychology. All must be employed in order to form a picture of the internal and external development of Primitive Christianity during Apostolic and post-Apostolic times. But when we try to understand the unity of this history, the inner principle of what takes place, our study cannot be merely part of the history of religion and culture, say of Hellenism, or the establishment of a religious-ethical ideal of personality in our own psychological terms. On the contrary, we shall describe the continued life and activity of Jesus in the Church, His Body on earth. The New Testament is an ecclesiastical book, and anyone using it to form and foster a private religion for himself abuses his Bible. He is extending his patronage to the view of Primitive Christianity which sees a choice of several types of religion : between Jesus and St Paul, the Synoptists and St John. A theology which sees Jesus as just an ideal personality cannot possibly teach the unity of the New Testament. Only if Jesus is presented in unity with the Church, His Body on earth, can the Gospel of the New Testament be seen and experienced as one and indivisible.

Harnack declared that there are two Gospels in the New Testament: the Gospel concerning the Father, and the Gospel concerning His Son, the Saviour. We have maintained that this is not so; there is only one Gospel in the New Testament. Furthermore, it is of essential importance to adhere to this view. But we can only adhere to it if we oppose dualist teaching. The fact of the unity of the New

Testament can be asserted in no other way than by rejecting the rationalistic view of Biblical history and surrendering to the eschatological interpretation. It is true that it can be made to seem scientifically plausible that Jesus, St John and St Paul stand on the same ground of eschatological reality. But the rationalist thinking of the West, with its characteristic conception of reality, is so deeply rooted in us, and so much governs our thought, that we must always make fresh attempts to liberate ourselves from it, and to gain such independence of it that we can read the New Testament aright. Western Christianity, and especially its Biblical theology, must learn the limitations as well as the advantages of its Greek intellectual heritage. It must hold together in its thought Jesus of Nazareth and the Christ of dogma and worship, and learn to see their unity everywhere in the New Testament. This lesson cannot be learned in solitude with the Bible, nor in the obscurity of a conventicle, but only in living communion with the Holy Catholic Church.

The problem of Primitive Christianity is that of *the unity of the New Testament*. This unity cannot be found by tracing, in the various parts of the New Testament, a common idea or ideal which may be more or less clearly recognized in and behind all the formulas of the Primitive Church if these formulas are only a religious and ethical "after-effects" of Jesus's religious and ethical personality. The ground of unity is the Lord Himself in unity with His Church. From this point of view the variety existing in the New Testament ought not to be a religious problem or an obstacle to faith; on the contrary, it is an enormous asset. It can and must be understood as such, if we recognize that in all the Scriptures the one Lord speaks through the one Church. After His departure He spoke and is ever speaking through the Church, the extension of His life, death and resurrection, which in all its varying forms is one with the living Lord through the Word, the Holy Spirit and the Sacraments, so that there is

One body and one Spirit,
One Lord, one faith, one baptism.

The problem of the unity of the New Testament is that of *the unity of the Church.* The old method of research which compared concepts, formulations, statements of faith and doctrines must be modified to show them as aspects of and insights into the common but richly differentiated faith and life of one Primitive Church. Then much greater consistency will be found than it was possible to discover previously. But, above all, the unity will be seen in multiplicity, and in that multiplicity will be found the evident token of the historical reality of the New Testament.

IV

THE CALLED AND THE CHOSEN

AN ESSAY ON ELECTION

Krister Stendahl

I

No one denies that the New Testament contains clear statements concerning divine election, and that foremost among these are the pregnant words of Jesus in Matthew xxii. 14: "For many are called, but few are chosen." It is therefore useful to discuss certain questions about the problem of election. In his recent book, *The Biblical Doctrine of Election*, H. H. Rowley points out what inadequate treatment this problem has received and continues to receive in practical as well as exegetical theology. The problem is usually relegated to the dusty realm of the history of dogma, and is largely ignored by Biblical theologians and in more general modern theological discussion.

The reason is that the idea of election is remote from modern thought and the more obvious problems raised in ordinary pastoral work. There are only two kinds of situation in which it naturally occupies the forefront of men's minds. The first is where a limited number of people who are confident of their own exclusive salvation withdraw from a lost world into an exclusive community of divinely favoured persons. The second is when it is believed that the promise of final triumph at the Last Day will be fulfilled within the lifetime of the present generation. These two factors—belief that only a select few can be saved, and the expectation of an imminent Second Coming—are the usual reasons for interest in the doctrine of Election.

Election not only raises difficulties because it is hard to reconcile with the language and thought of modern philosophy; the mutual relations of the Church and society may also tend to obscure it. In "established" churches, and in countries where the bulk of the population professes formal Christian faith, belief in election is sustained with the greatest difficulty.

Our examination of New Testament teaching about election must not be prejudiced by these facts. For the revival of scholarly interest is itself evidence that it is a cardinal element in the teaching of Holy Scripture. We may well agree with Professor Rowley when he writes, "Whether we like it or not, the doctrine of election is a Biblical doctrine, and whatever our view of its validity, it demands some attention from the student of the Bible." [1]

4 Ezra viii. 3 reads "many have been created, but few shall be saved", [2] a statement which Montefiore has characterized as "mournful and irreligious" [3]; while at the same time he points out the similarity and perhaps the dependence of our Lord's words in Matthew xxii. 14. Even if modern research, not least through the *religionsgeschichtliche*, has learnt to discount subjective considerations, no scholar can entirely escape the influence of his own personal point of view. Among the present generation we have noticed at least two reasons why the doctrine of election is discounted. Even Professor Rowley gives some evidence of apparently unconscious bias, despite the last words of his book, "This Biblical doctrine of election may be proclaimed without apology. . . ." [4] In his very reference to "*this* Biblical doctrine" he implies a degree of private interpretation of it.

When Rowley states as his main thesis that all Biblical election is election for service, he seems to supply a true interpretation of many texts. For his thesis is not only true of individuals; the group is also given tasks to perform. In such a way the character of the Old Testament Covenant

---

[1] Rowley, *The Biblical Doctrine of Election*, p. 15.
[2] I quote the Pseudepigrapha in the edition of R. H. Charles (1913) here and in the following pages.
[3] C. G. Montefiore, *Synoptic Gospels*, ii. (1927²), p. 290.
[4] *Op. cit.*, p. 174.

is made clear, as is the key idea of Israel as the centre from which Jahweh will save mankind, for "salvation is from the Jews" (John iv. 22). It is also evident that the election of the Apostles is connected with commission and service. The New Testament use of *diaconia* in connection with the Disciples is significant here. But for the actual words about election in Matthew xxii. 14 it is impossible to find a meaning other than salvation, or membership of Messiah's Kingdom. That this is the only true definition of election in the New Testament even Rowley would not deny, but his insistence on "service" undoubtedly lessens the offence and brings the doctrine into line with our present-day utilitarian presuppositions.[1]

But usually the main concern of commentators is with the purpose of the election doctrine, to establish its theological and psychological significance. With Augustine as well as Luther and Calvin it is said to have a twofold bearing, *contra superbiam et contra desperationem*. The doctrine of election becomes a way of understanding the sovereign grace of God. The faithful may also be encouraged by the description of it as divine comfort and consolation. But unless we are careful, we shall be led away from the doctrine of election as we find it in the Bible; and we must still ask why this doctrine of grace was worked out as a doctrine of election.

Returning to Rowley's discussion, we find him making an important reservation: "At the outset it must be made clear that I do not propose to deal with the theological question of predestination to salvation or damnation, to heaven or to hell. That is an entirely different question from the one that is before us."[2] But such a reservation, however convenient, may not be possible if the subject is to be fully discussed. Rowley aims, however, at a distinction of great significance: the frame of New Testament ideas is a philosophy of finality, not one of causality.

[1] Rowley's definition of election is partly explained by the fact that he really discusses the Old Testament and appends a chapter on the New Testament entitled *The Heirs of Election*, assuming immediate continuity without regard to the books of the Apocrypha.
[2] *Op. cit.*, p. 16.

E. Stauffer has thrown light upon the subject in his investigation of Paul's use of the conjunction *hina* [1]: "'Not leading hither, but directing thither' is the key to his thought" ("'Nicht Herleiten, sondern Hinfuehren' ist das Prinzip dieses Denkens," p. 241). The word *hina* epitomizes the problem of the plight of the world and God's intervention. Stauffer makes clear his meaning by citing Romans viii. 3 f., *. . . hina to dicaiōma tu nomu plerōthe en hēmin. . . .* The doctrine of election must be studied as part of this complex of ideas. When studying it in the first Gospel, one at once thinks of Matthew's formula *hina plerōthe to rhēthen. . . .*

Traditional Western doctrines of predestination merely answer the questions "how" and "why", and they belong to the causality type of thinking familiar in Western philosophy. Their concern is with the cause behind the world; the Bible is concerned with finality. It gives an interpretation of facts as a message of a revelation.

There is therefore a methodological issue of great importance in holding apart the problem of election and the "entirely different question" of predestination. But when O. Cullmann defines "election" in its New Testament sense as "the practical relevance-to-self (*Ichbezogenheit*) of the redemptive history," [2] "election" is in danger of being transformed into a synonym for "faith", instead of being of its own right a true *actus Dei*. The thought "that the number of the elect is determined" (*dass die Zahl der Erwaehlten eine bestimmte ist*) and that the Kingdom is prepared for the elect "from the beginning of the world" [3] requires a doctrine of election in terms of predestination. To reject predestination altogether is merely to obscure and distort the teaching of the New Testament.

Predestination causes difficulty because it is also necessary to assert man's responsibility. But man's responsibility is a paradox when placed beside any meaningful doctrine of

[1] *Hina* und das Problem des theologischen Denkens bei Paulus. *Theologische Studien und Kritiken*, 102 (1930), pp. 232–257.
[2] O. Cullmann, *Christus und die Zeit* (1946), p. 195. Engl. transl., *Christ and Time* (1951), p. 220.
[3] A. v. Harnack, *Terminologie der Wiedergeburt* (1918), p. 103.

election. Clearly the New Testament writers did not feel this difficulty in the same way as later theologians. Here again we can contrast two ways of thinking. Over against stringent logic stands Jewish thinking in images, where contradictory facts and conceptions can be put together in a kind of significant mosaic. Because of the peculiar character of Jewish thinking, the incompatibility of election and personal responsibility does not give rise to an intellectual problem in the New Testament.

One usually cites Philippians ii. 12–13, and calls attention to the fact that there Paul deals with the question in the much-quoted paradox, ". . . work out (*catergazesthe*) your own salvation with fear and trembling. For it is God which worketh in you both to will and to do of His good pleasure" (*eudocia*, cp. Luke ii. 14, Eph. i. 5, 9, where the idea of election is extended as far as the Creation). The commentators usually notice the paradox behind Paul's unqualified "*For* it is God . . ." But in his commentary on this passage, P. Ewald [1] points out incisively that the contrast Paul considers here is mainly that between *Paul's* supervising activity and *God's* work. Thus, it is not a question how man works alongside of a God "who worketh all in all". In the light of its context we may paraphrase the passage thus: When I was with you, you were zealous in your faith and obedience. Do not give in now that I am gone, for God is with you in my stead, and that is what matters, for He acts so that His plan of salvation may be accomplished. The paradox of election and personal responsibility is found here, but it does not become conscious, nor does it arrest the Apostle's attention. The passage is about a different subject altogether.

From this silence, however, it is not legitimate to draw the conclusion that the New Testament way of relating individual responsibility to God's act of salvation by means of election was fundamentally different from any at which we may arrive now. The difference lies in the manner rather than the substance of the thought.

The doctrine of election in the New Testament consists of

[1] Zahn, ed., *Kommentar z. N.T.*, XI (1923³), p. 136.

themes which can be illustrated by Matthew xxii. 14 and the statements in Ephesians i. 4 ff. about election in Christ. In the history of the doctrine of election Calvin is a central figure. P. Barth writes about Calvin's development of his doctrine of predestination: "It is the texts from Ephesians i and Colossians i that obliged him to make use of the idea of election in this part of his teaching (in the Institutes of 1536 about *Credo sanctam ecclesiam catholicam*). When he presents the New Testament reality of the Church, these texts supply him with the fundamentals of his doctrine of election—that is to say, of 'how men are elect in Christ by the mercy of God before the Creation of the world'." [1]

Election in Christ strictly implies that Christ is the truly Elect, as the beloved Son in whom God is well pleased. The faithful become participants in His election. "The idea of adoption of course remained after dogmatics no longer allowed it to be applied to Christ Himself," says Harnack,[2] dealing with the terms of individual election.

We here meet the doctrine of election in a sense which establishes that election and predestination are two different things. But even here—the reader must excuse my labouring the point—it should be observed how the idea of election in Christ may be watered down in apologetics. For example, P. Maury spoke on faith and election at the Calvinistic Congress at Geneva in 1936.[3] He made an interesting attempt to deal with modern man's difficulties about election. It contains such qualifications as: "There are no chosen and no repudiated, but there will be." "Try to replace the word 'before' (*vor*) by the two words 'independent of' (*unabhaengig von*), and you will come closer to the idea." But what smoothes the way for this interpretation of the Scriptures is the place given to election in Maury's systematic theology. Jesus Christ, we are rightly told, is the origin, cause and purpose of election. But we are left with nothing to say about the text to which we have drawn special

[1] *Theologische Aufsätze*, Festschrift Karl Barth (1936), p. 434.
[2] A. v. Harnack, *op. cit.*, p. 103.
[3] Later translated into German and published as *Theologische Studien*, Karl Barth, ed., 8 (1940).

attention, "For many are called, but few are chosen," which must in some way concern individual election.

A discussion about "Election in Christ" compels us to see in its true proportion the collectivism of the New Testament. On one hand, how meaningless Paul's agonized theodicy in Romans ix–xi would be, unless one could consider the question of the Jewish people as a whole apart from that of its individual members. What application would the ultimate salvation of all Israel have to St Paul's Jewish contemporaries who died without knowledge of Christ? The collective entities St Paul is considering occupy whole æons; the old Israel passes away, and out of it comes the Kingdom of God. The birth-pangs of the Messianic kingdom have already begun. Election in Christ not only constitutes a new society; its meaning is to be found in the new society, and not in the status of individuals. But on the other hand, what room, if this is so, can there be for the words, "For many are called, but few are chosen," or for a second Matthean saying with a strange, somewhat Johannine ring, ". . . Every plant, which my heavenly Father hath not planted, shall be rooted up" (Matt. xv. 13)? [1]

II

In his work on Jesus's Parables, Joachim Jeremias holds that conclusions or pronouncements in general terms have often been added to parables in order to round them off.[2] Jeremias sees in these additions an attempt by the early Church to modify the point and intention of the Parables. This tendency commences very early and is most noticeable in the Gospel of Luke. Matthew reaches the same goal by extensive allegorizing. "It is this tendency which finally

[1] Here we deliberately limit our study to Matthew. Other important passages about election are to be found in the Gospel of John. But there they form a complete unity and are so integral a part of the theology of St John that a discussion of them would necessitate a full-scale study of his theology. Election in the Fourth Gospel has been treated (with a survey of exegesis) by A. Corell, *Consummatum est*. Uppsala, 1950. (With an English summary.)

[2] Joachim Jeremias, *Die Gleichnisse Jesu* (1947), p. 71.

makes Jesus a teacher of wisdom and which . . . celebrated its greatest triumph at the end of the last century in Jülicher's interpretation of Jesus's Parables." [1]

The generalized *logia*-conclusions mentioned above can be conceived in different ways; for instance, as faithful summaries of the parables themselves, or as importing a completely new meaning. Greater support can be obtained for the opinion that we have in Matthew xxii. 14 an independent word of Jesus, the position of which is attributable to the evangelist. He has associated it with the description of a royal marriage and a man without a wedding garment. From earliest times importance has been attached to the paradox that the *one* man repudiated should be identified with the *many* reprobate. And if "the called" refers to the first part of the Parable, dealing with the many who were invited (in both cases the Greek is *clētoi*), then the conclusion must be that none of the called were chosen, as we read in Luke xiv. 24: "None of those men which were bidden shall taste of my supper." [2] If we are willing to assume that the final sentence was a traditional proverb, there is no reason why Jesus should not have appended it to His Parable. Nevertheless, probability confirms Jülicher's opinion: "This text of Scripture does not sound like a Matthean coinage; he has probably borrowed it from tradition, and in any case such a text agrees with Jesus's teaching; but Matthew has presumably inserted it here, because the Parable mentioned *clētoi* and illustrated the world of difference between receiving the Invitation and partaking of the Meal; the *gnomē* in verse 14 corresponded quite well with what he wanted to teach by the Parable: to partake in God's Kingdom involves more than the bare fact of an invitation." [3]

The independent character of verse 14 is illustrated by the reading of Matthew xx. 16, to be found in the Authorized Version; *textus receptus*, supported by the Western text,

---

[1] *Op. cit.*, p. 73.
[2] An obvious explanation without theological speculation is that our Lord speaks of one reprobate to secure greater emphasis—a device often found in the Parables.
[3] A. Jülicher, *Die Gleichnisse Jesu* (1899), II, p. 427.

repeats the saying here, so that the Parable of the labourers in the vineyard concludes with two pronouncements: (1) "So the last shall be first, and the first last"; and (2) "For many are called, but few are chosen." Even in Luke xiv, the parallel to Matthew xxii. 1–14, this saying has crept into some manuscripts; but there it has evidently been a case of the harmonization of the Synoptic material.

There are no real reasons to doubt that in Matthew xxii. 14 we have a "true saying of Jesus" as Jülicher is inclined to agree. R. Bultmann, who is a radical sceptic here, uses only general terms in discussing this passage, which he regards as a word of threatening (*Drohwort*). "One must realize that tradition has absorbed many statements of popular wisdom and piety, and it should be taken into account that tradition has been obliged to do so here and there by the action of Jesus in taking up or discussing such a saying. But even so, one must realize that many a saying has been adopted by tradition because of its own suitability and of its connection with the interests of the Church, and that it has not infrequently been composed for that purpose." The latter type includes Mark x. 31, with parallels in Matthew xx. 16 and xxii. 14, "if they are not traditional phrases of Jewish apocalyptic".[1]

The opinion that only a few shall be saved at the Last Day is not difficult to parallel in Jewish apocalyptic. It is a modification of the Old Testament doctrine of the remnant. 4 Ezra viii. 3, quoted above, is a good instance: "Many have been created, but few shall be saved"; compare vii. 49–61 and viii. 1: "This age the Most High has made for many, but the age to come for few"; 2 Baruch xliv. 15: "For to them shall be given the world to come, but the dwelling of the rest who are many shall be in the fire"; and 4 Ezra ix. 15: "There are more who perish than shall be saved." One may compare the rabbinic speculation, "And why was the future world created with the letter *yod*? Because the righteous men therein are but few" (Menahoth 29*b*).[2]

---

[1] *Geschichte der synoptischen Tradition* (1931²), p. 110.
[2] *The Babylonian Talmud*, Epstein's translated ed. (1948).

The antithesis of the few and the many is a main theme in Jesus's preaching; compare Matthew vii. 13 ff. and the question, "Will the saved be only few?"[1] which Jesus answers affirmatively, while turning it into a summons (Luke xiii. 23 ff.).

The few are called *hoi eclectoi* in complete agreement with the linguistic usage of Jewish apocalyptic, especially as we meet it in the Similitudes in cap. 37–71 of the Ethiopian Book of Enoch. One can compare, for example, the *Damascus Documents*,[2] where even the relatively rare thought of *non*-election is found clearly formulated: "For before the world was, God chose them not, and ere they were established He knew their deeds . . ." (p. ii. 7). It continues: "And the sons of Zadok are the sons of Israel called by name . . ." (p. iv. 3). Their numbers are determined (2 Bar. 30: 2, 75: 5), and their names are registered in books (cp. Dan. xii. 1; Enoch xlvii). In 4 Ezra we often notice at the same time a more qualified view, as for example viii. 55 ff.: "Therefore ask no more concerning the multitude of them that perish; for having received liberty they despised the Most High. . . . For the Most High willed not that men should come to destruction; but they, his creatures, have themselves defiled His Name. . . ."

That Matthew xxii. 14 has its real background in conceptions of this kind is confirmed by the fact that the term *eclectoi* in the Gospels is principally found in the apocalytic chapters of Mark and Matthew (Mark xiii. 20, 27, and Matt. xxiv. 22, 31). It is the elect who assemble from the four winds, and it is for their sake that the travail is shortened. The Western text prefaces *hoi clētoi* and *hoi eclectoi* with the definite article, which indicates that these are thought of as distinct groups (cp. Luke xiii. 23: *hoi sozomenoi*).

In his commentary, J. Weiss offers an illuminating interpretation of the concept of the few in Matthew xxii. "The idea is: *Because* they are the elect of God, they are created to

[1] Notice the definite article in the Greek text, *hoi sozomenoi*, from which it is evident that "the saved" is a technical term for a specific body.
[2] S. Schechter, ed., *Documents of Jewish Sectaries* (1910).

accept the Gospel; and from the fact that they accept it, one can infer that they belong to the elect. If this is an authentic saying of Jesus, and we have no reason to doubt it, we see that He Himself was resigned to failure with the multitude as to the inevitable. His task was, like a water-diviner, to find the *few* who, touched by His word, would meet Him with a childlike response and earnest repentance." [1] Weiss consequently describes Jesus's mission as the gathering of the few. Against the apocalyptic background this becomes credible, in spite of the modernistic speculation about His being resigned to failure.

On the other hand, a distinction between *clētoi* and *eclectoi* is made in Matthew xxii. 14, and is contingent upon the situation at the actual arrival of the Messiah. In Revelation xvii. 14 they are synonyms, just as there is no antithesis between them in Paul's description of the working of God's mercy in Romans ix. 29 ff. or between *clēsis* and *ecloge* in 2 Peter i. 10. An additional difficulty is uncertainty about Aramaic equivalents. K. L. Schmidt argues on such grounds that in this place *clētos* and *eclectos* have the same meaning and that the antithesis lies in a flat paradox: Many are called and yet only few are called, or, Many are elected and yet only a few. [2] In favour of such an interpretation the Midrash on Samuel viii can be quoted [3]: "Not every one who is near, remains near; not every one who is afar off, remains afar off. Some of the elect are rejected, and again restored, but there are also some of the elect, who, being rejected, are never brought near again." If a real identity exists between the terms one could just as well say, Many are chosen but few called; but this is hardly possible. Matthew must attach a special meaning to election, which is lost when *eclectos* becomes one of many synonyms for "disciple" and loses its meaning of one who is predestined.

Even if critical inquiry regards the saying mainly as a

---

[1] J. Weiss, *Die Schriften des Neuen Testaments*, I (1907), p. 368.
[2] K. L. Schmidt, *Theologisches Wörterbuch z. N.T.*, III, p. 496.
[3] Quoted in G. Dalman, *Jesus Jeschua* (1922), p. 205. Engl. transl. (1929), p. 228.

clue to the way in which Matthew understands the Parable, we must ask ourselves what light the context throws on the meaning of the saying. It will become obvious that *clētoi* is closely related to the four forms of *calein* in verses 1–10. According to Luke, who also uses *calein* to describe the invitation, the burden of the Parable is that none of the men who were called shall taste of the meal. The men originally invited have severally and collectively forfeited their invitation. The consequence is the same as in Matthew xxi. 28–46, as in the stories of the two sons and of the wicked husbandmen, and as generally in xxii. 1–10. Matthew xxii. 14 can be regarded as a suitable summary of the message of all these parables.

But what about verses 11–13 and the man without a wedding garment? [1] If we examine the last two sections of Matthew xxi. we find a treatment of one of St Matthew's most common themes, that of the necessity of *doing* God's will, of showing the fruit of God's Kingdom (*to thelēma tu patros poiein* (cp. vii. 21, xii. 50, and John *passim*; *poiein tus carpus*). To be sure, this *doing* must not be interpreted as a purely ethical term, but throughout Matthew there is a motif which stresses the importance of right action. The standing criticism of the Pharisees is: "They say, and do not" (Matt. xxiii. 3). Their actual righteousness is not so much perverted as insufficient (Matt. v. 20). For Matthew their disobedience is on a par with their rejection of the claim of Jesus to be Messiah, a claim which appears in Matthew above all as the proclamation of the perfect Law.

Here Jülicher's interpretation is sound: "When Jesus comes, it is not so much the publicans and sinners or the Gentiles who, according to Matthew, put to shame the Jews

---

[1] In the rabbinic version this Parable is complete and independent. Here it has another purpose. It teaches constant preparedness for death, especially by repentance. "Repent a day before your death. . . . Does a man know on what day he will die? . . . All the more let him repent to-day; perhaps he will die to-morrow" (Sabbath 135a, quoted by C. G. Montefiore, *Rabbinic Literature and Gospel Teachings* (1930), p. 310). The connection with repentance raises the question to what extent this text has been related in St Matthew's Church to the question of repentance. (Cp. xviii. 15 ff.) W. Michaelis discusses the problem in *Das hochzeitliche Kleid* (1939), pp. 68–70.

or the over-pious in Israel, but the righteous in truth put to shame the righteous in name. . . . In Luke a social, but in Matthew a moral revolution forms the last epoch in the history of the Kingdom of God." [1] When B. W. Bacon says, "He (Matthew) also appends in verses 11–14 a supplement in the interest of his favourite moral of good works," [2] we realize that this supplement shares the Matthean characteristics of the accompanying Parables.

We assume then that the "wedding garment" designates the quality of life appropriate to discipleship. This is undoubtedly in the main tradition of interpretation. It agrees with Revelation xix. 8, where the fine linen of the saints' garments is their "works of righteousness" (*n.b.* the Greek plural, *ta dicaiōmata*).[3]

Some examples from the Fathers will illustrate this. Irenæus [4] writes, "Yet again he showed that we must together with our calling be decked with works of righteousness, that the Spirit of God may rest on us, for this is the wedding garment, about which even the Apostle says: '. . . we would not be unclothed, but clothed upon, that mortality might be swallowed up of life'" (2 Cor. v. 4). Origen says, "He blames him for having ventured to come in without putting on [5] the wedding garment, of which virtue is the loom." Even from earliest times we find the rival interpretation of the wedding garment as Baptism, but this never appears in antithesis to the view which makes it the works of righteousness or of *caritas*. For baptism is not regarded as grace without the works of the law, but as consecration to effective righteousness.

In the tradition of Lutheran exegesis it has been zealously

---

[1] *Op. cit.*, p. 430.
[2] B. W. Bacon, *Studies in Matthew* (1930), p. 72.
[3] The Authorized Version has "the righteousness".
[4] Quoted from the *Ante-Nicene Exegesis of the Gospels*, ed. H. Smith (1928), v. pp. 19 and 25. It is to be noted, however, in this passage from Irenæus that "this" (Latin "*hoc*") does not refer directly to "the Spirit of God", but to the situation which reveals "the Spirit and works of righteousness". See *Contra Haer.*, IV: 36: 6, Migne P.G. VII.
[5] Greek *analambanein*. The term for putting on clothes, without implying a gift or gratuitousness. (Cp. Eph. vi. 13.) The quotation is from Origen's Comm. in Matthew xvii. 24, Migne P.G. XIII.

maintained that the wedding garment stood for imputed righteousness. People have cited the custom of a distinguished host's presenting his wedding guests with a garment, quoting the authority of Genesis xlv. 22; Judges xiv. 12; 2 Kings v. 22, x. 22; Esther vi. 8, viii. 15. There is no example from the time of Jesus to illustrate this custom, and such an important point cannot have been left to chance interpretation. We must not force the Parables to fit the requirements of a logic which is foreign to them. It rests upon the assumed question, Why could the host demand wedding garments? But the silence of the accused shows that this is not the point. The exegetical tradition we are criticizing goes back to Luther himself.[1] "The wedding garment is faith. . . . All the Fathers, Jerome, Augustine, etc. have discussed this passage and interpreted it as the garment of Charity. The poor men did not see how the Scriptures everywhere demand faith of all; if it exists, all that belongs to Charity follows as a matter of course. I believe this has happened because of God's wrath and indignation and that the Holy Fathers have not recognized and glorified the power and the effect of faith, although they knew that faith is the first requirement for salvation. Nowhere has any of them, in speech or writing, commended faith; all their writings point towards charity."[2] Thus Luther builds here upon mere generalities, and in more recent commentaries it is pretty generally agreed that the theory of a garment provided by the host must be given up. Even W. Michaelis,[3] although his interpretation of the passage is Lutheran enough, gives an explicit warning against such an exegesis of the garment.

That the early Church's word to describe the new life,

---

[1] Sermon, Nov. 2nd, 1522, *Luthers Werke*, W.A., X. 3, pp. 413:4–13, quoted from *Evangelienauslegung*, ed. E. Mülhaupt, II (1939–49), p. 729.

[2] Calvin takes an intermediate position when he writes: "As to the *wedding garment*, is it faith, or is it a holy life? This is a useless controversy; for faith cannot be separated from good works, nor do good works proceed from any other source than from faith. But Christ intended only to state that the Lord calls us on the express condition of our being renewed by the Spirit after his image . . ." (*Harmony of the Evangelists*, ed. W. Pringle (1949), ii. p. 171).

[3] *Op. cit.*, pp. 68–70.

caritas, is not ill-chosen is clear from a passage which Jülicher links in an interesting way with xxii. 11–13, namely xxiv. 12 f.: "And because iniquity shall abound, the love of many (*tōn pollōn*) shall wax cold. But he that shall endure unto the end, the same shall be saved." [1]

Naturally Jülicher also quotes Matthew xxv. Jews as well as Gentiles, publicans and harlots, must be taken to come into the presence of the Judge; but the point on which judgement turns is whether they have made themselves worthy by "deeds of charity". On the other hand, Jülicher points out that "the Kingdom is called *hetoimasmenē hymin apo catabolēs cosmu*: the text reads *hymin* rather than *tois dicaiois*, *tois eclectois*, of people coming to the feast in wedding garments. . . ." But when statements of this kind begin to carry Jülicher's thought towards predestination, he argues: "the man who wrote xxi. 33–46 (the wicked husbandmen) and xxii. 1–14 (the wedding feast) can never have thought of an irrevocable predestination for isolated individuals." [1] This, however, is by no means self-evident.

Matthew xxii. 11–13, which B. W. Bacon had characterized as an example of Matthew's "favourite moral of good works", is interpreted by C. H. Dodd as designed "to guard against the reception of the Gentiles into the Church on too easy terms" [2] (cp. v. 17–19, x. 5–6, xxii. 2–3). Even if this is really St Matthew's intention and if, as in Dodd, it is associated with the opinions of "the Judaistic opponents of Paul", it is nevertheless so completely merged with the whole Matthean conception of Jesus's message and work that it is an illustration rather than a special explanation of it.

If we interpret v. 11–13 as an epilogue (characteristic of the Matthean tradition) to the theme of the Messiah's calling, mission and reception in the world, then another problem is raised: why does Matthew associate his picture of works and charity with the doctrine of election? At the very point where we can rightly speak about his "favourite moral of good works", Matthew chooses to refer to election. But

---

[1] *Op. cit.*, p. 429.
[2] C. H. Dodd, *The Parables of the Kingdom* (1936²), p. 122.

what seems to us a paradoxical juxtaposition must have appeared to his contemporaries to be an obvious connection. In Jewish apocalyptic the works of righteousness are the distinctive mark of the elect.

Here it is sufficient to refer to the language of the Book of Enoch, where "elect", "righteous" and "holy" are synonyms, often in the juxtaposition "elect and righteous" (in some manuscripts "elect righteous"; see Charles's note to i. 1 with references to thirteen examples). In 4 Ezra the same view prevails with some modification. But divine approval is not obtained by the prayer of Ezra in 4 Ezra viii. 36, "For in this, O Lord, shall thy righteousness and goodness be declared if thou wilt have mercy on those that have no wealth of good works." The solution in 4 Ezra is rather that the unrighteous have themselves to blame (xiii. 60), and that the elect should not reflect upon the fate of others: "But do thou rather think of thine own case and search out the glory of them who are like thyself" (viii. 51). The Damascus Document also associates "righteousness" with a pronounced doctrine of election. (In this document the relation to the New Testament conception of "the remnant" is evident; see above, pp. 71–2.) The Damascus congregation could be called "the congregation of the righteous", a phrase which appears in Enoch also; and in Enoch lxii. 15 three points of importance to Matthew are interwoven: "And the *righteous* and *elect* shall rise from the earth. . . . And they shall be *clothed with garments of glory* (life)." It is in such a world of ideas that the Jewish concepts of election matured, so that we may rightly say that the two words "works" and "election" were synonymous, when Jesus the Messiah came as the Elect to gather the elect around Him.

In the New Testament a clear example of the relation of election and works is the catalogue of virtues in Colossians iii. 12, which begins with the words: "Put on therefore, as the elect of God, holy and beloved . . ." (cp. Eph. ii. 10). The same connection exists in the Apostolic Fathers, and in the catechetical teaching of the Church it becomes especially prominent. Matthew xxii. 14 is cited in the Epistle of Barnabas iv. 14. It is contained in an appeal and this is its context: "Let us become spiritual, a perfect temple of God. As much as in us lies, let us exercise ourselves in the fear of God; and strive to the utmost of our power to keep his commandments, that we may rejoice in his righteous judgement. . . . Take heed therefore lest sitting still, now that we are called, we fall asleep in our sins; and the wicked one gets the dominion over us and shuts us out of the Kingdom of the Lord. Consider this also, my brethren: although you have seen great signs and wonders done among the people of the Jews, yet notwithstanding the Lord hath forsaken them. Beware, therefore, lest it happen to us as it is written: Many are called, but few are chosen."

Some passages in 1 Clement teach the same thing, where in the introduction (i. 1) the dissensions in Corinth are contrasted with the status of the Corinthians as the elect. In terms which recall Philippians ii. 13, it is written, "Ye contended day and night for the whole brotherhood, that with mercy and conscience the number of his elect might be saved" (ii. 4), and "Let us therefore join ourselves to the innocent (*athōöis*) and righteous (*dicaiois*); for they are the elect of God" (xlvi. 4).

It is therefore no surprise when the sentence about the called and the chosen in Matthew becomes associated with the wedding garment. If we try to determine the relation between works and election which is implicit in such an association, then the great difficulty is, as we have repeatedly seen above, to let "election" keep its character of predestination, so that it is not just a synonym of "believer", "holy", "Christian", "disciple", etc. The identification may then rest *either* upon the subjective experience of human unworthiness and God's mercy, *or* upon the influence of a false imagery which evacuates the true meaning of the terms involved.

If we accept the identification, we shall be forced to see an essential contrast between Jewish apocalyptical pronouncements that the saints of the Last Days are predestined and

79

statements of a similar nature in the New Testament. But no such contrast can be justified by reading back into the Bible our own modern theologizing; this is no way to approach the problems of Biblical theology.

With due reference to Jewish apocalyptic, it should be possible to discuss the problems raised by human responsibility and works, and by divine election and grace, in such a way that a true account may be given of predestination. The elect are righteous and the righteous elect, because good works are the authenticating fruit of divine election.

Of course, the term "righteousness" gains a new and profounder meaning in the New Testament, which modifies its meaning in the Old. But the change is not from active righteousness to imputed righteousness, but from lower to higher, and so the principle of good works persists as a crucial teaching of Matthew's Gospel. For in the Church a life of higher righteousness is lived, and only one who participates in that way of life can belong to the elect. Matthew v. 20 is as important for the whole meaning of the Gospel as is the final division of mankind on the last day into good and evil. These two eschatological categories correspond to the few and the many, in accordance with the apocalyptic tradition. The insistence on a necessary performance of good works does not prejudice the predestinarian character of election. St Matthew's doctrine of election is an essential guide to an understanding of the nature of our election in Christ, by virtue of which the individual is brought into a relationship of faith with Christ and His Church. A collective election *in* Christ, which is not at the same time an individual election *to* Christ and the Church, does not do justice to the text, "For many are called, but few are chosen."

The most emphatic statement of election which Scripture contains is plainly not intended to offer comfort or to give faith an anchor beyond the veil. It is a word of warning and an explanation of the fate of those whom it rebukes. But the warning is not just emotive language culled from apocalyptic sources; the terms in which it is expressed must be allowed their literal force.

V

THE NEW EXODUS OF SALVATION ACCORDING TO ST PAUL

Harald Sahlin

THE DELIVERANCE out of Egypt through God's own marvellous intervention was seen more and more clearly by the Jews of Old Testament times as God's great act of election, whereby He chose Israel to be His peculiar people. Several Psalms bear witness to the fact that this historical event was understood to be of epoch-making significance for Israel. Since God had, through this act of deliverance, given powerful evidence of His intention to save Israel, it became natural for the Jews to consider the sacred story of the Exodus as a guarantee that God is perpetually active to deliver His peculiar people. Consciously or unconsciously they came to shape their anticipation of the great eschatological salvation through the Messiah according to the pattern of the historical Exodus under Moses. A striking instance of this is to be found in Deutero-Isaiah (Isa. xxxv and xl ff.) in the mighty prophecies which are essentially variations on the Exodus story.

Early Judaism increasingly understood eschatological salvation as a repetition, on a large scale, of the historical Exodus. The form that the ritual of the Jewish Passover, or *Pesach*, had come to assume unquestionably assisted this result. The *Pesach* festival, which had originally had a manifold significance, became in time simply an historical memorial of the Exodus from Egypt. This historical event was recalled in detail at every celebration of the *Pesach*; the feast was observed not only as an act of commemoration but still more as something which pointed forward to a new and still greater deliverance.

This typological correspondence between the Exodus and the Messianic act of salvation is often expressed in Rabbinic literature. A standing formula met with in several connections runs as follows: "As the first deliverer (*i.e.* Moses), so the last deliverer (*i.e.* the Messiah)." The Messiah was expected to repeat what Moses had done. Among other things, He was to send new plagues upon the oppressors of Israel, He was again to bring forth water out of the rock and to perform a miracle of manna. Like the deliverance from Egypt, the final deliverance would take place at the Passover. The Rabbis claimed justification for drawing a parallel between the first and the last deliverances even in what would seem to us to be inessential details. The starting-point of this parallel between Moses and the Messiah was found in Deuteronomy xviii. 15 and 18, where the Lord says to Moses, "I will raise them up a Prophet from among their brethren, like unto thee"—a passage which has traditionally been interpreted as referring to the Messiah.

The typological parallel between the historical Exodus and the Messianic deliverance, which was thus anticipated by Early Judaism, is also fundamental for the New Testament, and to a far greater extent than we generally realize. A rapid glance at the first and the last book of the New Testament will convince us of this. In the *Gospel according to St Matthew* Jesus is presented as the New Moses, in accordance with Deuteronomy xviii. 15 and 18. The first two chapters of St Matthew to a large extent correspond to Jewish legends concerning the birth and childhood of Moses. The Sermon on the Mount is the New Law given from the mountain by the New Moses. The ten miracles described in chapters viii–ix correspond to the ten plagues in Egypt, though antithetically; instead of judgements on the oppressors of Israel, they are acts of salvation on behalf of the new people of God. Further, the Gospel according to St Matthew may be divided into five distinct parts, viz., chaps. i–vii, viii–x, xi–xviii, xix–xxv and xxvi–xxviii, which correspond numerically to the five books of the Pentateuch. These brief indications will suffice. In the *Book of Revelation* there is an obvious parallel to the Exodus in the "sea of glass" (xv. 2) corresponding to the Red Sea; and those standing on the shore singing "the song of Moses and the Lamb" correspond to the children of Israel, who, after crossing the sea, sing the hymn of deliverance in Exodus xv. The seven vials of wrath in Revelation xvi are counterparts of the plagues of Egypt. Other parallels could be mentioned.

The typology of the Exodus was fundamental for the Evangelists, and supplied no merely accidental correspondence, which could have been dispensed with. This appears from the presence of the type in Deutero-Isaiah's prophecy "Prepare ye the way of the Lord", which is used in all the four Gospels to characterize and explain the significance of John the Baptist; he is the forerunner, who now inaugurates the new eschatological Exodus, which is to be fulfilled by the Messiah.

This may be sufficient to show clearly that a typological correspondence between the historical Exodus and the Messianic deliverance was not only generally accepted among the Jews in the time of Jesus, but was also taken for granted in serious theological thinking; Exodus typology was, in other words, of a dogmatic character. Consequently, it is only natural that we should also meet it in *St Paul*. To him, Exodus typology was clearly of fundamental importance, as we shall proceed to show.

In St Paul's Epistles there are in all about forty references, or allusions, to the history of the Exodus. Only a few of the main passages will be treated here. First we will turn to 1 Corinthians x.

The first fifteen verses of this chapter form an exposition of the Exodus story. We are reminded of the passage through the Red Sea, the miracles of the manna and of the water brought forth from the rock, as well as of the backsliding and idolatry during the journey through the desert. St Paul does not draw the attention of his readers to this story simply to produce examples from sacred history for purposes of edification, but because the Exodus story is of direct importance to his own generation. He writes (x. 6): "Now

83

all these things happened unto them for examples; and they are written for *our* admonition, upon whom the ends of the world are come." In order to understand how St Paul could thus apply the Exodus story typologically to his own age, let us think of the Jewish *Pesach* celebration. As we have mentioned, the feast of *Pesach* was celebrated principally in commemoration of the Exodus out of Egypt. Bitter herbs and unleavened bread were eaten to remind the people of their bitter bondage and of their hasty flight. This feast of commemoration was understood to imply that those who took part in it became one with the Exodus generation itself. In the *Pesach* ritual there is a passage which runs, "In every generation it is the duty of a man to imagine that he himself has come forth out of Egypt. It is written (in Exodus xiii. 8): 'This is done because of that which the Lord did unto *me* when I came forth out of Egypt.' God has not only delivered our fathers, he has also delivered us. It is written (in Deuteronomy vi. 23): 'And he brought *us* out from thence, that he might bring us in, to give us the land which he sware unto our fathers.' Therefore it is our duty to thank, praise, magnify and glorify Him who has done all these wonders for us and brought us out of bondage. . . ." Thus far the *Pesach* ritual. We would emphasize that when each generation celebrated *Pesach* it experienced in itself the deliverance out of Egypt. Hence it was quite natural for St Paul to consider the Exodus story as really written about his own generation, "He brought *us* out from thence."

Being a Jew, St Paul must have felt that in this sense he himself belonged to the Exodus generation. But as a *Christian* he must have had this feeling still more strongly. He knew that he belonged to the new eschatological Exodus under Jesus, the Messiah; and, in his opinion, this New Exodus of Salvation was a complete typological counterpart of the ancient, historical Exodus, only on a larger scale and in a more profound sense. The typological parallelism must therefore be nevertheless antithetic; the new Exodus is in every aspect far superior to the old. (A similar antithetic comparison is, as we know, made in the Epistle to the

Hebrews between Christ as High Priest of the New Covenant and the high priest of the Old Covenant.)

St Paul writes (1 Cor. x. 1 f.): ". . . all our fathers were under the cloud, and all passed through the sea; and were all baptized unto Moses in the cloud and in the sea." It seems as if there had been present in the mind of St Paul the purpose of setting forth another and better baptism, the baptism unto Christ, over against the "baptism unto Moses". He does not do this, however, and his mind reverts to the divine food and drink of the desert wanderings, to the manna from heaven and the water springing from the rock. This food and drink are made to serve as typological counterparts of the elements of the Eucharist. Accordingly, after a lengthy excursus on the backslidings of the desert generation (x. 5–15), the Apostle proceeds in verse 16 ff. to speak of the Eucharist. Hence, the train of thought regarding baptism unto Moses, started by St Paul in the beginning of the chapter, is not continued here. In order to find its sequel we must turn to a different context. However, before doing so, we will examine another passage in the First Epistle to the Corinthians.

In 1 Corinthians v. 6–8 St Paul writes, "Know ye not that a little leaven leaveneth the whole lump? Purge out therefore the old leaven, that ye may be a new lump, as ye are unleavened. For even Christ our passover is sacrificed for us. Therefore let us keep the feast not with old leaven, neither with the leaven of malice and wickedness; but with the unleavened bread of sincerity and truth." Here St Paul distinctly alludes to the celebration of the *Pesach*. The purging out of all that could be designated leaven, and the sacrifice of the *Pesach* lamb, were the principal elements of the feast. The parallel of the leaven is quite boldly applied by St Paul so as to make it represent all that pertains to the "old man"; the Christians themselves are "unleavened", and must therefore be completely free from all "leaven". Again, as regards the *Pesach* lamb, St Paul says that Christ is the true Paschal Lamb of the Christians—a thought which is also expressed in the Gospel according to St John. Furthermore, this quotation shows that St Paul is thinking of the redeemed condition of the Christians as a true and everlasting *Pesach* feast. The true Paschal Lamb was once for all sacrificed, and Christians are, as such, "unleavened" and free from all defiling leaven. The thought of the Christian life as a continuous Passover is also Biblical. The purpose of God's command to Moses to lead the children of Israel out of Egypt is that they may hold the Passover. In Exodus iii. 12 it is written, ". . . and this shall be a token unto thee, that I have sent thee: When thou hast brought forth the people out of Egypt, ye shall serve God upon this mountain."

But as the keeping of the Passover, the institution of which is recorded in Exodus xii, is the *immediate* purpose of the Exodus, so the divine celebration of it remains the *ultimate* aim. Hence *Joshua* celebrates the Passover as soon as he had led the children of Israel across the Jordan into the promised land (Josh. v). And King Josiah's reformation is manifested by a great "passover unto the Lord" (2 Kings xxiii. 21 ff.).[1] We find the thought of an ideal celebration of the Passover in the New Testament, above all in Hebrews xii. 18 ff., and also in the two last chapters of the Book of Revelation. In the first passage, the Church of Christ is described as the typological counterpart of Zion—the goal of the desert wandering of the people of God; while Israel still remains, figuratively speaking, at Sinai, the true people of God have reached the Heavenly Jerusalem of the everlasting worship of God. In the last two chapters of Revelation the same thought is expressed in a rather different manner. Here too the Heavenly Jerusalem, which is at the

---

[1] Occasionally this ideal service is thought of, not as a *Pesach* feast, but as the Feast of Tabernacles, which in a certain degree is related to the Passover. Thus, the great religious service which was held at the consecration of Solomon's temple is a Feast of Tabernacles (cf. 1 Kings viii, esp. v. 2). The same is true regarding the consecration of the new Temple related in Nehemiah viii., as well as the eschatological worship recorded in Zechariah xiv. 16 ff. But when the prophet Ezekiel describes the ideal Temple and its cult (Ezek. xl–xlviii), he has the celebration of *Pesach* in mind. This is evident, among other things, from the fact that his great vision of the Temple, according to Ezekiel xl. 1, occurs "in the beginning of the year, in the tenth day", *i.e.* the very day when, according to Exodus xii. 1 f., the *Pesach* feast begins.

same time identical with Paradise, is thought of as the ultimate goal of the New Exodus of Salvation and the *Pesach* feast is transformed into what is called the marriage of the Lamb.

The two passages from the First Epistle to the Corinthians which have been discussed above show that St Paul regards the status of Christians as the result of a new Exodus, the typological counterpart of the Exodus out of Egypt. What event, however, is to be regarded as the starting-point of this new Exodus, and the counterpart of the actual departure from Egypt? The answer can only be the death and resurrection of Christ. This is obvious from Romans vi. 3 f., where we read, "Know ye not that so many of us as were baptized unto Jesus Christ were baptized unto his death? Therefore we are buried with him by baptism into death: that like as Christ was raised up from the dead by the glory of the Father, even so we also should walk in newness of life." The status of the Christian depends solely upon the death and resurrection of Christ. But the passage quoted also indicates that man partakes of Christ's death and resurrection by baptism. In order to understand this line of thought we must first explain Jewish teaching about baptism.

First, it may be asked, What was John the Baptist's intention in his baptism? We read about him that he "preached the baptism of repentance for the remission of sins" (Mark i. 4; Luke iii. 3). This translation, however, is scarcely correct. Instead of "the remission of sins" it probably ought to read "the putting away of sins". By receiving the baptismal bath, men were to wash away their sins. Baptism was to lead to "repentance", or conversion to God. Those who received baptism were thought of as abandoning their old sinful lives, and emerging from the water as new and righteous creatures. Of course, the water was not thought of as having any *magical* effect; but baptism was in a genuinely Biblical sense a "sign". Nor was it merely of *symbolical* significance, but possessed rather the character of a *sacrament*. John preached this baptism of

87

repentance because he knew that he was the forerunner of the Messiah. His divinely appointed mission was to "make ready a people prepared for the Lord" (Luke i. 17). Only a righteous people could receive the Messiah; but Israel was not a righteous people. It is true that, in an external sense, the Jews were sons of Abraham, but they did not reveal a righteousness befitting true sons of Abraham (cp. Matt. iii. 7–10; Luke iii. 7–14). True repentance was therefore necessary. This is what John the Baptist proclaims, not only in words but also in deeds, by performing a sacramental baptism of repentance for the putting away of sins.

What was the source of John the Baptist's baptismal teaching? It is neither necessary nor correct to look beyond Judaism, *e.g.* to the baptismal movement of the Mandæans. The baptism of John is entirely founded on the Old Testament world of ideas, and should be understood in the following way. When God, through His servant Moses, called Israel out of Egypt in order to make it the people of His covenant, Israel had to pass through the Red Sea to arrive at Sinai, where the covenant would be established. Thus Israel was "baptized unto Moses in the sea", as St Paul says in 1 Corinthians x. 2. This baptism implied the putting away of all Gentile ways of life, all this being left on the western shore, or perishing with the Egyptians in the sea. Israel arising out of the sea was a purified people, worthy of adoption into the covenant of God. A Rabbinic saying runs: "When Israel received the Law at Sinai, he was a new-born child, one day old." Israel could now begin a new life. It is true that the period of wandering in the desert after the covenant at Sinai was filled with sin and back-sliding (cp. again 1 Cor. x. 5–15), but it was nevertheless capable of interpretation as an ideal time of close fellowship with God, when God Himself led his people by the pillar of cloud and the pillar of fire, and was present in the Tabernacle.

The purpose of the baptism of John is a sacramental regeneration of the people, to prepare the New Exodus of Salvation under the Messiah. Consequently, he appears in the desert, and there summons the people to him. That is where the New Exodus is to begin. Symbolically, baptism itself implies a new passage through the Red Sea, whereby Israel is again cleansed from its heathen ways of life and from its sins, and its people become true sons of Abraham, worthy of receiving the Messiah on His arrival. Baptism, like the crossing of the Red Sea, was a *collective* act; a great many people let themselves be baptized: according to Mark i. 5 "all the land of Judæa and they of Jerusalem". As regards the performance of baptism, we must, of course, not think that John himself poured water on every individual. The people, by the order of John, no doubt descended into the water of the Jordan or any other convenient stream and then ascended again on the other side, just as the children of Israel marched through the Red Sea by the order of Moses.

Thus, the baptism of John was a sacramental representation of the historical Exodus of Israel and, at the same time, an introduction to the New Exodus of salvation. In John the Baptist the prophecy of Isaiah, "The voice of him that crieth in the wilderness, Prepare ye the way of the Lord", was fulfilled.

Before we proceed to Christian baptism we must first discuss *proselyte baptism among the Jews*. When a non-Jew wished to be converted to Judaism, as seems to have been common in New Testament times, it was not sufficient for him to adopt the Jewish faith. There were certain rites that had to be fulfilled, and particularly circumcision, proselyte baptism, and sacrifice in the Temple at Jerusalem. *Circumcision* was, ever since the time of Abraham, the covenant sign of Israel, so it was naturally an indispensable condition of becoming a proselyte. As regards *proselyte baptism*, its background was Exodus typology. It was not enough that the non-Jew had received circumcision; he also had to be associated symbolically and sacramentally with the historical acts through which the election of the Jewish people took place. Like Israel he had to depart from Egypt and march through the Red Sea to be received into the covenant of God in the desert. Proselyte baptism is held to represent the passage through the Red Sea before the covenant at Sinai.

The fundamental idea of proselyte baptism is the same as that of John's baptism. The proselyte who had received proselyte baptism could celebrate the Passover like other Jews, and join in the words, "We have all been in Egypt and marched through the Red Sea". He had, that is to say, been enrolled as a full member of the people of God. And this fact was expressed by the *sacrifice* which the proselyte performed in the Temple.

To describe this entering into the body of the people of God there was a special term: "being brought under the wings of the *Shekinah*". The *Shekinah*, the holy Presence of God, is an important element in the theology of Judaism. As God's peculiar people, Israel is thought of as being "under the wings of the *Shekinah*", and within the sphere of holiness. The non-Jew who is incorporated by proselyte baptism into the people of God, shares the holy status of a dweller under the wings of *Shekinah*. This expression recalls the time of Israel's wanderings in the wilderness, when God's *Shekinah* as the pillar of cloud rested over the tabernacle and upon the whole congregation. In Rabbinic times it came to be taught that, during their wanderings in the wilderness, the congregation of Israel was constantly surrounded on all sides by a curtain of clouds, or enveloped by a single great cloud. We read, for instance, in a passage of the *Pesiqta*: "For what people did I cleave the sea? To what people did I give the manna? . . . What people was it that I enveloped with the cloud of glory?" This Rabbinic teaching explains how St Paul can speak of a "*baptism* in the cloud." In the passage already quoted (1 Cor. x. 1 f.) he says, "All our fathers were under the cloud . . ., and were all baptized unto Moses in the cloud."

Furthermore, it is of great importance that proselyte circumcision together with baptism should have been regarded as a new birth. By virtue of his incorporation as a proselyte into the body of the people of God, a convert to Judaism began a new life, a life in holiness. Hence a common expression in Rabbinic times runs: "He who becomes a proselyte is like a new-born babe." We recognize this thought in the Rabbinic saying quoted above: "When Israel received the Law at Sinai, he was like a new-born child, one day old." Similarly, those who had received the baptism of John probably considered themselves to be a new-born, holy people. The thought of rebirth through baptism was well known in those times. It is met with also in the New Testament in connection with *Christian baptism*, which we will now proceed to discuss.

St Paul nowhere presents any clear exposition of the meaning of Christian baptism. From the two passages quoted above, 1 Corinthians x. 1 f. and Romans vi. 3 f., however, we can form an idea of St Paul's understanding of it. Jesus Christ is the New Moses, effecting the New Exodus of Salvation. The actual starting-point of this work of salvation by Christ is in His death and resurrection. *Thus the death and resurrection of Christ have the same meaning for the Church as the crossing of the Red Sea has for Israel.* As through circumcision and proselyte baptism the Jewish proselyte is incorporated into the people of God and becomes a partaker in God's act of salvation as recorded in the Exodus narrative, and primarily in the crossing of the Red Sea, so the *Christian* proselyte, receiving Christian baptism, becomes a partaker of Christ's act of salvation, His death and resurrection. As the Jewish proselyte becomes by baptism *one* with the Exodus generation, so the Christian through baptism becomes *one* with Christ in His death and resurrection. This is what St Paul says in Romans vi. 3–5: "Know ye not, that so many of us as were baptized into Jesus Christ were baptized into his death? Therefore we were buried with him by baptism into his death: that like as Christ was raised up from the dead by the glory of the Father, even so we also should walk in newness of life. For if we have been planted together in the likeness of his death, we shall be also in the likeness of his resurrection." The language in verse 3, "Know ye not . . .", indicates that St Paul refers to matters well known to his readers. A more thorough explanation of the meaning of Christian baptism must of course have been included in the instruction of catechumens; therefore St Paul did not think it necessary to give a detailed explanation of the nature of baptism in this passage or in 1 Corinthians x, where it would otherwise have seemed natural for him to do so.

The individual who through Christian baptism has "died and been raised again with Christ" may consequently be said "to be in Christ"; he is virtually incorporated into the body of Christ. Hence, by the Pauline formula "to be in Christ" there is meant, strictly speaking, no kind of mystical union with Christ; it states the purely objective fact that through baptism a person has been "planted together with Christ" (Rom. vi. 5). To St Paul this was evidently an objective reality just as it was an objective reality to Judaism that through circumcision and proselyte baptism the proselyte was admitted into the Exodus generation and becomes a partaker of its salvation.

And furthermore, just as the Jewish proselyte is "brought under the wings of the *Shekinah*", and having entered the sphere of holiness is himself holy, so the Christian becomes "holy" through baptism. He now belongs to the *true* people of God. Consequently this holiness is of an objective and theological nature. When St Paul calls the Christians "the saints", he does not claim that they live a morally perfect life; he only says that, because they are baptized, they belong to the body of Christ. On the other hand, their holiness should be *manifested* in a holy way of life. Consequently St Paul, no doubt in accordance with Jewish practice, is inclined to make use of paræneses, or exhortations, whenever he is thinking of baptism. Thus quite characteristically we find, both in Romans vi and 1 Corinthians x, such paræneses in a baptismal context. St Paul argues in this way: As you *have become* holy by your baptism, you must *lead a holy life*. Or, as he says in 1 Corinthians v. 6–8, because the Christians are the people of the New Exodus and so eat the unleavened bread of sincerity and truth, they must purge out the old "leaven", and as in Romans vi. 4 f., "walk in newness of life". (Cp. also Rom. vi. 22 f.)

As already mentioned, the Primitive Church regarded Christian baptism as also a new birth, or alternatively as a new creation (cp. Tit. iii. 5; John iii. 3–8; 2 Cor. v. 17; Gal. vi. 15, and other passages). Similarly, both the baptism of Israel in the Red Sea and proselyte baptism were described as a new birth. Thus, in this connection also the language of a New Exodus of salvation occurs in the theology of the Primitive Church.

So far we have discussed the subject of baptism. We shall now proceed to the *Eucharist*. St Paul says remarkably little about it. Whereas baptism, although not expressly mentioned, obviously underlies lengthy sections of St Paul's Epistles, the Eucharist is discussed in only two passages, 1 Corinthians x. 16–21 and xi. 20 ff.

The liturgical and theological position of the Eucharist in the Primitive Church is still extremely obscure. One difficulty is met with at the very starting-point. Was our Lord's Last Supper, as recorded by the three Synoptists, a real *Pesach* meal, or was it, as in the Gospel of St John, celebrated on the previous evening? This question has been the subject of lively discussion. Lately, in a series of discussions of this problem, *Joachim Jeremias* has energetically maintained that the Last Supper of Jesus was actually a *Pesach* meal. The fourth Gospel has transformed tradition in order to present Jesus as the true Paschal Lamb, sacrificed at the same time as the *Pesach* sacrifice of the Jews. The difference in chronology is, however, of little importance. The important fact is that Jesus stands out as the true *Pesach* sacrifice. The words of institution—"this is my body", "this is my blood"— point clearly enough to the Jewish *Pesach* ritual. The distribution of the bread and wine implies that the communicants become partakers of the propitiating power of the sacrificial death of Jesus.

Accordingly, it seems most natural to regard the Christian Eucharist as a continuation of the *Pesach* celebration of the Jews. Christ is our Paschal Lamb, and we, His Church, continually celebrate the Passover (cp. 1 Cor. v. 7 f.). Hence there is a connection between our Eucharist and the *Passover* of the Jews. The Eucharist, too, has Exodus typology. Thus it is easier to understand the relation between Baptism and the Eucharist. *Baptism* signifies the beginning of the New Exodus of salvation in Christ. It denotes the incorporation of a member into the body of Christ. Consequently baptism, like Jewish circumcision, is a non-recurrent act because the baptized person becomes once for all a partaker through baptism of the saving work of Christ and enjoys communion in Christ's life. The *Eucharist*, on the other hand, corresponds to the *Pesach* meal of the Jews. It is a remembrance of the death and resurrection of our Lord, and in consequence a renewal of His act of salvation so that we in our own generation benefit by His saving act. But at the same time the Eucharist, exactly like the *Pesach* meal, points forward to the Parousia (cp. 1 Cor. xi. 26: ". . . till he come") and to the final eschatological goal which the New Exodus of salvation will one day reach. The Eucharist is the viaticum of the pilgrims of the New Exodus and the antitype of the manna and water from the rock in the first Exodus (cp. 1 Cor. x. 3 f., 16 f.). Consequently it belongs to the nature of the Eucharist, as well as the Jewish *Pesach*, to be continually repeated; not once a year, however, but more frequently. The Church of Christ celebrates an everlasting Passover—a thought which we have previously found in St Paul (1 Cor. v. 7 f.), and which is further developed in Hebrews xii and Revelation xxi f.

Thus we conclude that the New Exodus of salvation determines the thought of St Paul as well as of the entire Primitive Church. The New Testament can, as a whole, be regarded as a detailed fulfilment of the types of the Old Testament Exodus, God's great act of salvation for the people of His election. Baptism and the Eucharist as they appear in St Paul must be related to this typological background if we are to understand their full meaning.

Modern theology has not been sufficiently alive to the importance and meaning of Exodus typology. Yet it has always survived in the liturgical worship of the Church, and the fine collect for Easter Sunday in the Swedish rite will serve to illustrate the wealth of its theological significance:

94

"Almighty and Eternal God, Who didst deliver Thy people out of Egypt by the hand of Thy servant Moses, and didst command them to observe the Passover annually and eat the paschal lamb: bring us also, O heavenly Father, out of the spiritual Egypt, and make us partakers of the true Paschal Lamb, Thy Son Jesus Christ, our Lord, who this day hath conquered death, and opened unto us the way to eternal life, and now liveth and reigneth with Thee and the Holy Spirit, for ever and ever. Amen."

VI

THE MINISTRY IN THE NEW TESTAMENT

Harald Riesenfeld

NEW TESTAMENT research in the last few decades has
led us to revise the picture of Primitive Christianity
which was still current far into the twentieth century.
Until quite recently it had been considered primarily as a
doctrine or a way of life greatly superior to all philosophical
systems or religious movements which vied for souls in the
Hellenistic Mediterranean world, but, like them, essentially
a product of the spiritual currents in its environment.
Christ Himself was seen as the great Teacher and the Ideal
Personality, and attempts were made to divest Him of the
supernatural trappings which were thought to be due to the
arbitrary interests of a popular tradition given to legendary
embellishment. The first Christian generation was envisaged
as consisting of men who had been united by their common
enthusiasm for a purified and deeper religion. But among
them there were men who, with the help of conceptions from
other forms of contemporary belief, remodelled Christ's
simple gospel in the complex of dogmas and organization to
which the books of the New Testament already testify, and
which was to assume an even more dogmatic character at a
later date.

But we have now learnt, or been forced to learn, that the
truth was other than this; the beginnings of Christianity
were less simple and humanitarian, and were not to be
explained as the evolution of more elementary into more
complex forms. Christ's own message has proved to have
perspectives of cosmic and universal range, and to be
stamped by the eschatological situation and by the thought
of man's redemption from the powers of evil into a community

whose foundation God had long prepared and foretold through His prophets. Christ, the Son of Man and not only the Ideal Man, joined issue with Satan, sin and death, to gather about Himself the chosen Remnant, and by His life sealed the creation of a new age, a new world, and a new humanity.

This reassessment has also affected the question of the nature and essence of the Christian community. It is not surprising that a period which was mostly concerned with the individual and his religious psychology was not able to see in an organization like the Church anything more than a group of believers united by external circumstances. The following priorities were assumed: the individual existed before the local congregation, and the local congregation before the universal Church. In the same way, ecclesiastical offices or ministries were regarded as purely peripheral to Christianity, and were concerned solely with administrative duties and the maintenance of order. It was thought that the Spirit and the enthusiasm marking the oldest phase of the Church did not fundamentally need any forms or defined channels for their outward manifestation. The theory was that an initial spontaneity had gradually yielded to the necessity of having a cohesive and regulated organization, but that this was primarily of an administrative or judicial nature which gave it something of a secular stamp. Regular meetings and the practical needs of community life called for the institution of certain offices. But it was only when the anticipated return of Christ did not happen, and the Church began to establish itself in this world, that the ministries began to be accepted as something essential to it. The result was a wide variety in the organization of the Church, based solely on considerations of practical expediency. The monarchical episcopate was believed to be a late product of this evolution, visible in St Ignatius (*i.e.* at Antioch) at the beginning of the second century A.D., but not complete before the end of the century. The process by which the ministry—finally divided into the episcopate, the presbyterate and the diaconate—was held to be essential to the Church and given a theological interpretation, was regarded as a distortion of the original nature of the Church.

In recent years our view of the Church has undergone considerable change, as a result of important discoveries—or rediscoveries—made in connection with Christology. The key to the origin and nature of the Church has been found to lie in Christ's own awareness that He was the Messiah or the Son of Man, coming to gather and redeem the People of God. Round Him, and among those whom He called to follow Him, the Kingdom of God took shape. There is reason to suppose that Christ did not base His entire teaching on the supposition of an immediate Parousia; there are sayings which imply an interval between His death and His return on the Day of Judgment. The institution of the Eucharist is one of the signs that He expected the new way of life, embodied in and about His person, to continue during an interim period. The Church was part of our Lord's deliberate purpose; it continues the eschatological community of men which He gathered about Him during His life on earth. Because of this, even after His Resurrection Christ still works among mankind and offers them a way to salvation through their earthly condition. Therefore the Church, created by Christ Himself, universal and yet appearing in the world in visible form, is prior to the local congregations. In order to understand what the Church offers to mankind, we must first ask ourselves what significance Jesus attached to the idea of the Son of Man for the life and salvation of the People of God.

An attempt to learn a little more about the public offices or ministries in a Church thus conceived poses the initial question whether these offices too did not originate and take root in Christ Himself, and whether they are foreshadowed in the community of the redeemed, the New Israel, that appeared about Him. The part played by the Apostles suggests that this was so. They exercised a prominent ministry in the Primitive Church, as we know, but still earlier we find the most characteristic group of Apostles, the Twelve, as disciples of Jesus during His earthly life. Even then, in the eschatological community around Christ, they were fulfilling certain functions.

Here it may be appropriate to make a slight digression. We know now that the term "apostle", so common in the New Testament, is the Greek translation of the Hebrew word *shaliach*, which means "envoy" and, in a somewhat transferred sense, "fully authorized agent" or "representative". Among the Jews this word denoted a number of functions of a legal or religious nature. A representative of this kind could negotiate on behalf of the person he represented, and even contract a marriage. The Sanhedrin in Jerusalem empowered its envoys to co-ordinate the Jewish calendar throughout the Dispersion; and later on the patriarchs in Jamnia appointed delegates to inspect the administration of the dispersed congregations. On this analogy a prophet is thought of as sent out by God and therefore as invested with special authority. The saying found in later Jewish literature that "a man's deputy (*shaliach*) is as himself" is enough to show that this term is a specialized one, which derives its significance from the context in which it appears. The same is true of the New Testament Apostles; the name "apostle" does not in itself express any definite function; it states that its bearers act on the orders of, and in a similar way to, the person who sent them forth. This consideration encourages us to move our investigation back a stage and begin with Christ, to discover which of His functions could be transferred by His authority to those whom He chose as His representatives.

Here we are helped by the Synoptic tradition, which gives us a picture of what happened when Jesus sent out His twelve disciples during His ministry in Galilee (Matt. x. 1 ff.; cp. Mark iii. 14 f., vi. 7; Luke ix. 1 ff.). He charged them to go about and preach there by proclaiming the message, "The Kingdom of Heaven is at hand", in the same way as He Himself proclaimed it. Further, He gave them power to cast out unclean spirits and to cure all manner of disease. That the individual disciple is to be considered as Christ's *shaliach* is expressly affirmed in such a statement as, "He that receiveth you receiveth me, and he that receiveth me receiveth him that sent me" (Matt. x. 40). The deputed disciples exercise a function which in certain respects resembles Christ's own Messianic function. For Christ in His turn regarded Himself as sent to fulfil a mission which had been given to Him from above. In view of this analogy, it seems fitting not only to speak of the task or mission of the *disciples* in the proclamation of the approaching Kingdom of God, but also to regard *Christ* as having a special mission with its necessary authorization; which means that He was the first to bear office in the new people of God. We are therefore justified in beginning our investigation of the ministry with Christ Himself.

Let us take a line which in the course of the last few decades has shed much new light on our understanding of Christ's life and work, and pose the following question: What are the implications of Christ's unmistakable claim that He was the Messiah, or the Son of Man? In the light of ideas current in Palestinian Judaism, we can definitely say that both the Messiah and the Son of Man are indissolubly linked with the concepts of the Kingdom of God and the People of God. The Messiah was thought of as the Ideal King, but a king must naturally have a kingdom to govern and a people to rule over.

It was the same with Christ. His person cannot be separated from the kingdom which was given to Him. It is true that He could say that His Kingdom was not of this world (John xviii. 36), but nevertheless it was present in this world; it was in His person and everywhere He went, it manifested itself through the power in His words and deeds, it forced itself on mankind and faced them with the final decision. Visible and evident also was the conflict into which this kingdom entered with a power of another kind, that of Satan, which was revealed in sickness and affliction, poverty and want, misfortune, sin and death. In this conflict between two kingdoms, concrete proof of their relative strength was given when demons were driven out, diseases healed, the dead brought to life, and other mighty deeds performed before marvelling humanity. Nor can the concept of the People of God be divorced from the person of Christ. It does not primarily apply to the Israel according to the flesh to which He belonged and in which He grew up; it applies in the first place to the New Israel which He founded, represented and gathered about Him. It is true that He preached a message and communicated a body of teaching, but His activity has not been sufficiently defined if we call Him simply a prophet or a teacher. In His person, and in the band that followed Him, we see the marks of a people, the People of God, which lives in the way that He laid down in His teaching on the Kingdom of God. Here, within reach, was the righteousness after which the old Israel strove in vain. And here the twelve disciples had the function of being the new tribes of Israel in germ.

However, it must also be remembered that Jesus was not only what we might venture to call the local centre of the Kingdom of God and the People of God on earth. He was, also, the One who maintained them by His personal ministry. His word cast out unclean spirits and forgave sins. His hand raised the sick and the dead. Moreover, it was through Him alone that men were given membership of the People of God. For without Him they were nothing but a lost and deserted multitude, "as sheep having no shepherd" (Matt. ix. 36). But he sets them in another way of life: "Come unto me, all ye that labour and are heavy laden, and I will give you rest. Take my yoke upon you, and learn of me . . ." (Matt. xi. 28 f.). All this He could say and achieve, because He was sent by God and endowed with divine authority radically to change the condition of mankind. He was God's representative before men, and men's representative before God.

Here a long perspective opens backwards in time. The very words "People of God" bring before us the long history of Israel which was in various ways the necessary and intended preparation for what, in the fullness of time, Christ was to bring. Israel had been a Holy People since the days of Abraham and Moses, because God had called them, given them a share of the promise and established the Law, made a Covenant with them, and led and maintained them through His representatives the patriarchs, kings, priests and prophets. But in spite of this, Israel was forced in the course of its long history to realize that the fullness was still to come. Eschatology became an increasingly prominent element in Jewish religious thought; there grew up a conviction that the future would bring a new and better age. What was wanting? What was it that made the people of the old Covenant but a shadow of the true People of God? The deepest reason was of course the disobedience and the apostasy that over and over again frustrated the fulfilment of the Covenant with its conditions and promises.

The whole of Israel's history reflects the conflict between the rule of God and the imperfect submission of the people. The Old Testament and the writings of Judaism show how this discord also manifested itself in the annual pattern of religious life, which was dominated by the struggle between order and chaos. At the beginning of a new year God created order and unity, and thus renewed the Covenant and the promises—but the year ended in apostasy, divisions and quarrels. It was useless to rely on the signs of unity which God had given to His people: circumcision, the Law and the Temple. For the heads of Israel who were charged with the oversight of its religion and who represented the people before God and God before the people, were themselves divided, and unable to sustain the unity of the people. Later, Judaism reckoned three fundamental offices, those of king, priest and prophet—a triad which seems to have ancient precedents. We see them distinguished from one another by the sheer current of events, a monarchy before the Exile, high-priesthood after it, a graded priesthood additional to both, and different forms of prophecy from age to age. It was only in extravagant eulogies and in eschatological speculations that these offices were envisaged as united in single persons. No doubt the very assignment of these offices and of their authority to different persons is evidence of the imperfection and disharmony which make perfection

and unity seem an unattainable ideal. But a final unity
was prophesied and longed for; it was to come with the
Messiah.

Now when in veiled terms but with eloquent eschatological symbolism Christ called Himself the Messiah, He
was consciously following the ideas developed in the Old
Testament and in Judaism. It was not only that He applied
to Himself single prophecies in the Scriptures; the fundamental ideas of the Old Testament found in Him their
explanation and their full expression. He embodied the
fullness of the Kingdom of God and of the People of God;
in Him, disobedience and apostasy were unthinkable.
Therefore He had been entrusted with all power and all
authority. He had within Himself the fullness of the
Spirit, and so was able to perform miracles. He communicated revelation which was far beyond everything which
there had been in the Old Testament, but which none the less
conformed to what was written there. He gave the final
Law. He made atonement for the sins of His people with a
sacrifice that rendered superfluous all the worship of the
Temple at Jerusalem. He set himself at the head of His
people, and knew Himself to be the Judge who would come
again in His glory on the Last Day to divide the good from
the evil. Round Him the New People was gathered,
represented by the twelve disciples. The number twelve
indicates that the age of salvation has come, when the tribes
are no longer scattered. He became the centre of unity,
for there was an indissoluble bond between Him as Messiah
and His followers. He had come for their sake, and they
formed a real community or people through Him. The
Spirit which was poured out on human beings, the message
proclaimed among them, the forgiveness offered to sinners,
the whole reality of salvation manifested in many particular
ways, cannot be divided from Christ's person, because they
became accessible only through Him. In Him the Kingdom
of God was active upon earth, and consequently those who
followed Him became a people of whose unity and continuance He was the guarantee.

The metaphor of the vine and the branches (John xv. 1 ff.) helps us to illustrate this relationship. The tree or the stem and the branches are for one another, and otherwise would have no reason to exist. Nevertheless, it is plain that the tree is at the same time the source of life, "for without me ye can do nothing" (John xv. 5). This metaphor is also significant in that it makes us see the Kingdom of God as a living organism, as do the other metaphors used by Christ in His teaching; here it will suffice to refer to the comparison with the grain of mustard, which is the least of all seeds, but when it grows it is the greatest among herbs (Matt. xiii. 31 f.). St Paul, in his turn, uses the metaphor of the body and its members to describe the Church (Rom. xii. 4 ff.; 1 Cor. xii. 12 ff.). It is naturally risky, when expounding these metaphors, to talk in terms of an organism in the sense of Greek philosophy, but their New Testament context shows that, for the New Testament writers, the use of the metaphor of a plant or a body involved, to some extent at least, an argument from its structure and function. A tree consists of trunk and branches, a body of head and members; that is their *structure*. The branches of the vine bear fruit by virtue of the life which comes to them from the stem; the members of the body are dependent both on each other severally and on the body in its entirety; that is their *function*. One further point can be clarified with the help of one of the parables quoted. Even to the Eastern mind it must have been clear that there is a connection between the seed and the plant. With our way of describing the relationship between the Messianic circle round Christ and the Church after His death, we should use the word "continuity". For there must be some equivalence in structure and function between the band of disciples gathered by Christ on the one hand, and the Church on the other.

In the New Testament Christ is only once called an apostle (Heb. iii. 1), a word which, as we have seen, derives its significance from the Hebrew *shaliach*. But we have already had reason to state that Christ was aware of being sent by the Father with absolute authority to carry out a mission (Matt. xi. 27; John xii. 44 f.). His place in the structure of the Kingdom of God was that of head and mediator. His function was to bring to men the blessings of the Kingdom of God. He did this by preaching the Gospel, performing mighty deeds, gathering and leading mankind, forgiving them their trespasses, giving them the Bread of Life and, not least, serving them, interceding and laying down His life for them. St Justin Martyr is the first Christian writer who expressly mentions that Christ held the three ancient offices known from Judaism, of King, Priest and Prophet; nevertheless the New Testament already contains several passages which make it clear that the Christian Church from early times regarded Christ in these rôles. There is no doubt that He Himself identified His person with these traditional offices. The peculiarity of His fulfilment of them is not only that He does not assume His official functions openly; this is in keeping with the mystery that surrounds the whole earthly life of the Messiah. Rather, according to the unanimous testimony of the New Testament, the difference is that Christ is King in a higher degree than any mortal ruler; He is the perfect King, who refuses to follow the pattern of the rulers of the world (Matt. iv. 8 ff.; cp. Luke xxii. 25 f.; John xviii. 36 f.). Similarly, the idea forming the main subject of the Epistle to the Hebrews, that Christ is the real High Priest, is hinted in many other books of the New Testament; His own words and actions show clear associations with the Jewish cult. The same is true of the conception of Christ as Prophet; He is the last and greatest Prophet (John i. 45; Acts iii. 22 f.; cp. Deut. xviii. 15, 18).

The unity and the fullness become evident in the fact that it is not possible, in Christ's person and work, to separate the different offices. They are combined. We need only recall the description of Christ's suffering and death; it is impossible to draw a line between the humiliated and victorious King and the High Priest who sacrifices himself, or between both of these and Christ's office as Prophet. Whether we proceed from the Jewish idea of the three offices, or presuppose a more complicated relationship of public functions and ministries, it is plain that in Christ we are confronted with a synthesis, based on traditional ingredients and creating a central headship or ministry which maintains the eschatological community. When we embody the conception of ministry in the person of Christ, a further point emerges. An office, at all events when it is duly exercised, exists not for the sake of the holder, but to uphold the community which it serves. "For even the Son of Man came not to be ministered unto, but to minister, and to give his life a ransom for many" (Mark x. 45).

This ministerial function of Christ among the People of God is brought out in a series of images or metaphors which He Himself used in His teaching. They reveal in a lucid way the intimate relationship between the Messiah and His followers; they also stress His active rôle and their dependent position.

Let us begin with the image of the *household* or the *kingdom*, which recurs with a number of variations. It is for the lord of the house to give to those entrusted to his care "meat in due season" (Matt. xxiv. 45). There is an association here with the eschatological meal, so that the features of householder and king are combined. Because associations of this sort are always fluid, there is no hard-and-fast line between God and Christ as the king or the householder; but this does not detract from the significance of the image, since Christ always acts on His Father's behalf. Do we not see how the images of "Kingdom of God" and "Kingdom of the Messiah" merge into one another? "A certain man made a great supper and bade many", writes St Luke (xiv. 16 ff.), while in St Matthew (xxii. 1 ff.) it is a King who prepares a marriage feast for his son. It is true that the festival supper is not an ordinary household meal; but even so the host at the festival performs the functions of the householder. In a symbolic way Christ acts as a host or householder at the miracles of the feeding of the multitudes (Mark vi. 35 ff., viii. 1 ff.), where He gives them that followed Him the Bread of Life (John vi. 51). He also teaches them to pray, "Give us this day our daily bread" (Matt. vi. 11).

The parable of the labourers in the vineyard (Matt. xx. 1 ff.) is similarly based on the relationship between the house-holder and his servants. We must also notice the important fact that there can be only one lord of the house or the kingdom, as is emphasized by the words: "Every kingdom divided against itself is brought to desolation; and every city or house divided against itself shall not stand" (Matt. xii. 25 ff.).

Thus, the passages which we have quoted express the view that the whole conduct of domestic economy depends on the householder; it is the master of the house who assembles his household or his guests, and gives them what they need.

Another image which recurs in Christ's teaching is that of a *building* which is set up, which rests on foundations, or which is being completed. Here, He often makes an association with the Temple, by which is meant the new Temple which will replace that of Jerusalem, and which is not made with hands. Within three days Christ will Himself build this new Temple (Mark xiv. 58; John ii. 19 ff.). But He does not only regard Himself as the builder, He often makes no distinction between the new Temple and Himself. The Messiah dwells among His own, as God once dwelt in the Tabernacle (John i. 14; cf. Rev. xxi. 3). Alternatively, He elsewhere describes Himself as the most important or pre-eminent part: "The stone which the builders rejected is become the head of the corner" (Mark xii. 10); this quotation from Psalm cxviii. 22 refers to the key-stone in the great arch above the entrance to the Temple. The parable of the house built upon a rock (Matt. vii. 24 ff.) does not, it is true, make any direct mention either of the Temple or of Christ Himself; here, it is primarily Christ's words which are likened to the foundations of the building. Nevertheless, there is surely a close association between the person of Christ as the foundation and His words. In its different presentations the image expresses how that which holds the whole together is an integral part of the building and has its particular function which cannot be dispensed with if the building is to stand.

From the Old Testament has been inherited the metaphor of the *shepherd* and his flock which is used in conjunction with the idea of a king and his people. God Himself is the true shepherd of Israel (cp. Ps. xxiii; Isa. xl. 11), but the human leaders of the people are also given this title (Jer. xxiii. 1 ff.; Ezek. xxxiv.). The mission which Christ fulfils towards His own is in no small measure illuminated by the shepherd metaphors which He applies to Himself. The Good Shepherd is the Leader of His own; the sheep follow Him, and He finds pasture for them. This Shepherd does still more, for He gives His life for His sheep; and He is the guarantor of unity: "There shall be one fold and one shepherd" (John x. 1–16; cf. Rev. vii. 17). The metaphor has further aspects. The shepherd who tends his flock as a whole nevertheless knows each single sheep, and seeks it when it has gone astray (Matt. xviii. 12 f.; cp. xii. 11 f.); but he does not withhold His stern justice when He divides the sheep from the goats (Matt. xxv. 31 f.). Once again, however, the key thought is that the shepherd is necessary to the existence of the flock. And a parallel is drawn; without Christ in His Messianic office, mankind are "as sheep not having a shepherd" (Mark vi. 34). Christ's humiliation and death are adequately characterized by the Old Testament text: "I shall smite the shepherd, and the sheep shall be scattered" (Mark xiv. 27).

Other similar images may be mentioned here. We recognize from the Old Testament the description of God as the keeper of the vineyard (Isa. v.), or the *gardener*, planting the Garden of Eden with the Tree of Life and Knowledge (Gen. ii. 8 ff.). Christ considers Himself as the Tree of Life: "I am the true vine, and my Father is the husbandman" (John xv. 1), but He can also say of mankind: "Every plant, which my heavenly Father hath not planted, shall be rooted up" (Matt. xv. 13). Christ Himself also assumes a more active rôle when He stands before the fig-tree—a variant of the Tree of Life—and curses it because it has not borne fruit in the time of the Messiah (Matt. xxi. 19 f.); in Luke xiii. 6–9 we have a similar idea in the form of a parable. A kindred image is that of the *sower*, which Christ uses with an obvious reference to His own person (Mark iv. 3 ff., 26 ff.). And if Christ is not Himself designated a *fisher*, He is none the less, as the Messiah, implicitly such when the Kingdom of Heaven is likened to a net that is cast to gather mankind (Matt. xiii. 47 ff.). He also calls disciples from their nets by the Sea of Galilee to make them fishers of men (Matt. iv. 18 f.); He tells Peter to take up a fish (Matt. xvii. 27); and after His Resurrection He directs how the disciples are to cast their nets (John xxi. 1 ff.). Nor is Christ ever called a *pilot*. But if we remember the story of the stormy passage of Gennesareth, which the Primitive Church took at an early date to symbolize the ship of the Church, it is clear that Christ Himself guarantees the safe course of the boat (Mark iv. 35 ff.). Finally, there is an Old Testament image which expressly sets forth the close bond between God and His people: the *bridegroom* and the bride. God's relationship with Israel is exemplified as a marriage (cp. Hos. ii.), and the bridal mysticism of the Song of Songs arises from ancient symbolism. Christ deliberately takes up this metaphor, and he indicates His own person when He speaks of the bridegroom who has come (Mark ii. 19 f.), or who still taries (Matt. xxv. 1 ff.). This symbolism subsequently reappears in the Apocalypse, when the writer sees the marriage of Christ with the heavenly Jerusalem, the glorified Church.

These images variously set forth Christ in His Messianic activity as the founder and sustainer of the People of God. Its structure can be most simply defined by saying that it consists of men gathered by the Messiah around Himself. And the different functions which the Messiah fills in order to sustain the People of God entitle Him to the name of steward or minister. The relationship between Christ and His people which is expressed in the metaphors we have mentioned is already implicit in the figure of the heavenly "Son of Man" described in the Book of Daniel (vii. 13 ff.), and afterwards in Judaism, above all in the Books of Enoch. There we plainly see the indissoluble connection between the Saviour and the body of the redeemed. This would seem to

justify the claim that our examination of the metaphors in
the Gospels has not been irrelevant to our attempt to discuss
the relation of Christ's person and achievement to the
Ministry.

At this point it is appropriate to turn our attention to the
disciples. As already mentioned, the description of how
they were sent forth during Christ's ministry in Galilee
reveals striking resemblances between the Master's activity
and that of the Twelve. They are His representatives;
and the Synoptic Gospels are faithful to this idea in confining
their use of the term "apostle" mainly to those occasions
when the disciples leave Christ to go on special missions
(Matt. x. 2 ff.; Luke vi. 13 ff.), or when they return to Him,
as deputies ought, to render an account of their doings
(Mark vi. 30; Luke ix. 10). The Fourth Gospel does not use
the word "apostle", but the term is unmistakably implied
when Christ says, "As thou hast sent me into this world,
even so have I also sent them into the world" (John xvii. 18).
When the disciples go forth, invested with power or authority
(Matt. x. 1), they act in the same way as Christ Himself:
they proclaim the coming of the Kingdom of Heaven, they
work miracles by casting out devils and healing the sick, and
they spread the peace which is the mark of the Messianic
kingdom (Matt. x. 1–15). To receive or reject one of the
disciples is the same as to receive or reject Christ (Matt.
x. 40; Luke x. 16). As the Messiah, Christ is filled with the
Spirit which speaks through Him and gives power to His
actions. But the disciples also have a share in the same
Spirit: "For it is not ye that speak, but the Spirit of your
Father which speaketh in you" (Matt. x. 20). After the
Resurrection, which was followed by the gift of the Spirit
to the Church in full measure, Christ equips His disciples
with the power for their missionary activities: "Receive
ye the Holy Ghost. Whose soever sins ye remit, they are
remitted unto them; and whose soever sins ye retain, they
are retained" (John xx. 22 f.). Normally, the power to
remit sins belonged solely to God; the very fact that the
Messiah claimed to have this power was a scandal to Christ's

contemporaries (Mark ii. 7). It must therefore have seemed all the more remarkable that Christ delegated to His disciples so crucial a function, and that He delivered to them the keys of the Kingdom of Heaven, the power to admit or to refuse to admit men to everlasting life (Matt. xvi. 19, xviii. 18). We can consequently say that the promised Kingdom of God is found where Christ is physically present, and that it appears wherever the disciples go forth on the Master's mission. For they do not do anything on their own initiative; they act exclusively in the name of Christ, that is to say, with His authority (cp. Mark xvi. 17). "The disciple is not above His master" (Matt. x. 24); it is the Master who acts perpetually through the disciples whom He sends forth.

It is not only His full power and authority which the apostles share with Christ, but also His service and His suffering. Because the Son of Man has come to serve and to lay down His life, He exhorts His apostles by saying, "Whosoever will be great among you, shall be your minister, and whosoever of you will be the chiefest, shall be servant of all" (Mark x. 43 f.). The washing of feet, which takes place at the Last Supper, is for the disciples an initiation into service: "For I have given you an example, that ye should do as I have done to you" (John xiii. 2 17). To represent Christ means to be like Him, to become as He was, not in some novel way which they devise for themselves, but by letting His mission speak through their whole course of life. As Christ's path ended upon the Cross, so must each disciple take up his cross and follow Him (Matt. x. 38). The disciples will be attacked and persecuted, they will encounter death, because their commission from Christ is a thorn in the flesh of mankind, "And ye shall be hated of all men for my name's sake" (Matt. x. 22). But there is no other way than this; "It is enough for the disciple that he be as his master, and the servant as his lord" (Matt. x. 25).

As envoys of Christ and as bearers of His authority, the disciples present the Kingdom of God to men in a concrete form by proclamation and instruction, by performing miracles and by giving help, and by the active pursuit of service. But it is plain that "disciple" in this sense does not include everyone whom Christ has called to communion with Himself and to participation in the Kingdom of God; it applies only to those whom He invested with a special mission within the eschatological community. There is no doubt that an office or ministry is in question here. At the same time, this office is entirely subordinate to Christ's own place and function in the Kingdom of God. This in itself really indicates the relation of Christ's own ministry to the Ministry which He institutes. This is a point about which there has been much confusion. We all rightly feel that Christ is unique, and infer that if *He* held an office, then a similar office cannot be held by men, however full of grace they may be. Our mistake here is to equate Christ with ordinary men, thereby making Him no more than a man, even if the greatest of men. But the Biblical view of the Messiah or the Son of Man, which without doubt was Christ's view too, is other than this. The divine Redeemer is more than human, not least by virtue of the fact that He embraces all humanity in His person. His Being is not only individual but also corporate. Against the background of the Old Testament Christ stands out not only as an individual figure, but also as summing in Himself the "remnant" of the Chosen People (cp. Isa. x. 21). In the New Covenant, He is the "first-fruits" who includes in Himself all the new People of God (cp. 1 Cor. xv. 23). Only if we grant this will Christ's words about the Son of Man's redeeming sacrifice be comprehensible; in it, both the Johannine "mysticism" (*e.g.* John xv. 4 ff.) and the baptismal theology of Paul (Rom. vi. 3 ff.) have their source. It is equally applicable to the Christian ministry. Seeing that Christ, as the Messiah, holds an office in the community which He founded and supports, the offices of His appointed ambassadors are contained in His own person and functions. Therefore He Himself works in them and through them; the body functions because Christ's own office is imposed upon and entrusted to mortal bearers who, through this call and this charge, become one with Him for the showing forth of His works. This is illustrated in the answer which Christ returns to Peter's question as to what reward the disciples shall have for forsaking all and following the Master, "When the Son of man shall sit in the throne of his glory, ye also shall sit upon twelve thrones, judging the twelve tribes of Israel" (Matt. xix. 28). The power to be Judge on the Last Day is accorded only to God or His Messiah. It is unthinkable that the apostles should on that day be empowered to exercise any judgment of their own; the purpose of the image is to show that Christ the Judge is active in His apostles and that they exist to mirror Him. Thus Christ's ministry is a shared ministry.

That this is not an extravagant line of thought is clear because the metaphorical language which has been used to illustrate Christ's function in the eschatological community is used also of His representatives, both in Christ's own words to His disciples and in the writings of the Early Church about the apostles or other ecclesiastical officers.

If God Himself, or Christ as the Messiah, is to be regarded as a householder or as the King of a kingdom, the disciples, acting in Christ's absence, are stewards who have full authority to take charge of the household or kingdom in their lord's place and on his behalf, and are responsible for the people of the house, to give them their daily bread and cater for all their needs. "The Son of Man is as a man taking a far journey, who left his house and gave authority to his servants, and to every man his work" (Mark xiii. 34). The conduct of the unjust steward is possible only if he had unlimited authority, so that the changes he made in the sums owed were legally binding (Luke xvi. 1 ff.). But despite his powers, the steward is always in a subordinate position and answerable to another; that is why we read that when the day of reckoning comes, he must give an account of his stewardship. "After a long time the lord of those servants cometh, and reckoneth with them" (Matt. xxv. 19; cp. xviii. 23). The function of the true steward is epitomized in the words, "Who then is the faithful and wise servant, whom his lord hath made ruler over his household, to give them meat in due season? Blessed is that servant, whom his lord when he cometh shall find doing so" (Matt. xxiv. 45 f.). The keys signify authority over that which is locked. In the Jerusalem of the kings, the chief butler carried a key as the symbol of the power of his office over the royal palace and its treasure (Isa. xxii. 22). In Jewish belief, God had reserved for Himself the keys of life, of the repository of rain, of the womb, and of the abiding-place of the dead. As the Son of God, Christ has the same power to open and shut the way to the human race (Rev. i. 18, iii. 7). When He says to Peter that He will give him the keys of the Kingdom of Heaven, He is delivering to him far-reaching powers: "Whatsoever thou shalt bind on earth shall be bound in heaven: and whatsoever thou shalt loose on earth shall be loosed in heaven" (Matt. xvi. 19). The disciple, then, is entrusted with the mission of judging and regulating mankind's admission to the Kingdom of God, and the same authority is also given to the whole body of the Twelve (Matt. xviii. 18; cp. ix. 8).

Just as Christ is the stone which holds the new Temple together, or which is its foundation, so St Peter in his capacity of apostle is the rock on which the Church of Christ shall stand (Matt. xvi. 18). Christ's mode of expressing Himself here is genuinely Palestinian; our thoughts are led to Mount Zion, on which the Temple of Jerusalem rested. The image might have been applied to the Messiah's own person, but instead, He confers upon the apostle a function which is Messianic in the sense that it is to be exercised in the Church of Christ, and that its power and meaning come from Christ. As to the metaphor, this saying of Jesus bears a striking resemblance to the parable of the house built upon a rock (Matt. vii. 24). The house which is built upon rock, the new Temple or Church, will defy the powers of chaos in the same way as the house withstands the beating rains: "The gates of hell shall not prevail against it (the Church)" (Matt. xvi. 18).

The disciple also assumes the part of shepherd. It is his task to follow the Master and go "to the lost sheep of the

house of Israel" (Matt. x. 6) and gather them into safe
keeping in the Kingdom of God. The last chapter of St
John's Gospel tells of the Risen Lord's thrice-repeated
charge to Peter to be a shepherd to His sheep (John xxi. 15 ff.).
This is where this disciple is definitely made an apostle. The
condition is that he shall love his Lord and therefore not
glorify himself at his Lord's expense; the consequence of his
mission will be that "another shall gird thee, and carry thee
whither thou wouldest not" (*ibid.* v. 18). His activity or
office is one with the ministry of Christ. And in a similar
way, Christ uses words descriptive of His own function when
He says that He will make the disciples fishers of men
(Matt. iv. 19; cp. John xxi. 4 ff.).

Passing now from the Gospels to the Acts of the Apostles
and the New Testament Epistles, to see what they tell us
about the ministry in the early Church, we are struck by the
evident continuity between the time of Christ's first sending
out of His disciples and the activities of the various officers
after Easter and Pentecost. As the Kingdom of God formerly
took shape wherever Christ worked in Galilee and wherever
His disciples went in His service, so now the Church exists
in all the places which Christ's ambassadors have reached
on their missionary travels, and where they have set up
Christian communities. The expansion and continuance of
the Church depend on the men who represent Christ, and
first and foremost on the apostles. We shall not here try to
discuss the difficult question of what relation the men
known as apostles bore to one another; we know that the
pre-eminent ones were the Twelve, Paul, and James the
brother of our Lord. But we should like to point out some
things which they had in common. Among these was a
consciousness of vocation, which gained its form from the
shaliach institution, and its content from the fact that Christ's
own activity continues in His Church. Therefore the
apostles acted with an authority which was entirely derived
from the commission which Christ Himself had given them.
This is clear from the description of St Peter's leadership in
the Church of Jerusalem as we find it in Acts, and it comes

out in St Paul's description of himself at the beginning of his Epistles, *e.g.* "Paul, an apostle (not of men, neither by man, but by Jesus Christ, and God the Father)" (Gal. i. 1). After Christ's death the Kingdom of God still continues to reveal itself, not as an impersonal power, but by choosing as its instruments men who work in Christ's place and in His name.

This authority is accompanied by the power of effectively preaching the Gospel and performing the miraculous acts of the Kingdom of God. "And with great power gave the apostles witness of the resurrection of the Lord Jesus; and great grace was upon them all" (Acts iv. 33). St Paul speaks both of the authority "which the Lord hath given us for edification, and not for your destruction" (2 Cor. x. 8; cp. xiii. 10), and of the grace which has been given him and of which he sees positive proof in the success of his ministry (Gal. ii. 9; cp. 1 Cor. iii. 10). The power given to an apostle is sometimes represented as the result of a pouring-out of the Spirit with which the apostle, like the Messiah, is endued from above. We need only recall the account of the Pentecostal miracle in Jerusalem (Acts ii. 1 ff.), and the description of the continued activity of the apostles, where they are described as bearers of the Spirit to a special degree. St Paul, too, can commend his authority with words such as these: "I think also that I have the Spirit of God" (1 Cor. vii. 40).

The miracles which are related to have taken place in the Apostolic Age should therefore be regarded as a continuation of Christ's own ministry. St Paul claims that Christ has worked through him "by word and deed, through mighty signs and wonders, by the power of the Spirit" (Rom. xv. 18 f.) because he is an apostle. "Truly the signs of an apostle were wrought among you in all patience, in signs, and wonders, and mighty deeds" (2 Cor. xii. 12). The Acts emphasize that many wonders and signs were done by St Peter and the Twelve (Acts ii. 43, iv. 30). There are two fairly full accounts of acts of healing (*ibid.* iii. 2 ff., ix. 32 ff.), and there is even a raising from the dead (*ibid.* ix. 36).

But it is quite clear that all this takes place in the name of Jesus Christ and by His power (*ibid.* iii. 6, iv. 10, 30, ix. 34). The following account shows the degree to which an apostle was considered as being invested with divine authority, and how power seemed to radiate from him: "They brought forth the sick into the streets, and laid them on beds and couches, that at the least the shadow of Peter passing by might overshadow some of them" (*ibid.* v. 15). St Paul, too, is presented in a similar way later in Acts; he performs signs and miracles (Acts xiv. 3, xv. 12), heals (*ibid.* xxviii. 8), and raises a man from the dead (*ibid.* xx. 7 ff.). A similar, though even more miraculous, picture of Early Christianity is afforded by the longer ending of the Gospel of St Mark (xvi. 17 f.). Similar to this is an apostle's ability to communicate blessing and peace; there is more in the salutations with which St Paul begins and ends his Epistles than benevolent wishes and hopes.

But even here, authority and power are balanced by the obligation to serve. Characteristically enough, the position of one of the Twelve is expressed by the two words "ministry and apostleship" (Acts i. 25). The duties of the officers of the Church find practical expression in tasks such as serving tables which the apostles, and those whom they in their turn appoint, have to perform when the congregations are gathered together to break bread (*e.g.* Acts vi. 1 ff.). This apostolic function calls to mind Him who at the Last Supper said to His disciples, "For whether is greater, he that sitteth at meat, or he that serveth? is not he that sitteth at meat? but I am among you as he that serveth" (Luke xxii. 27). St Paul, who is usually well assured of his own authority, declares that he has made himself servant to all (1 Cor. ix. 19) and abased himself (2 Cor. xi. 7), that he might indeed be a minister of Christ (*ibid.* v. 23). Because of Christ's example, suffering unto death is a necessary part of an apostle's vocation. (2 Cor. iv. 10, xii. 10).

The imagery associated with ministerial functions also helps us to grasp their continuity. The apostle is the steward of the mysteries of the Kingdom of God, which have been

entrusted to him that he may deliver them to mankind.
"Let a man so account of us, as of the ministers of Christ, and
stewards of the mysteries of God" (1 Cor. iv. 1; cp. ix. 17;
Col. i. 25). He holds an infinitely important and responsible position in Christ's household, the Church; it
engages his whole loyalty, but it also gives him the right to
speak and act in Christ's stead (2 Cor. v. 20). When Paul
says that "it is required in stewards, that a man be found
faithful" (1 Cor. iv. 2), he knows within himself that the
day approaches when the steward must render his account.

The image of a building, which Early Christianity applied
allegorically to the Church as the new Temple, is used with
different shades of meaning. It has been established that
Christ is the foundation on which this Temple is raised,
"For other foundation can no man lay than that is laid, which
is Jesus Christ" (1 Cor. iii. 11). He also has a unique
function as the chief corner-stone (1 Pet. ii. 4 ff.). But it
can equally be said that Christianity is built on the foundation
of the apostles and the prophets, Christ Himself being the
chief corner-stone (Eph. ii. 20). In the Apocalyptic vision
of the heavenly Jerusalem, the twelve apostles form the
foundation stones of the city wall (Rev. xxi. 14, 19 ff.).
Further, the image can be modified to show the actual
laying of the foundation. God has laid Christ as the
foundation of the Church (1 Pet. ii. 6), but Christ in His
turn can include His representatives in this function, as when
St Peter is called the rock on which the Church will be
erected (Matt. xvi. 18). The particularized character of
each apostle's activity in this connection can be deduced from
a similar statement of St Paul: "Yea, so have I striven to
preach the gospel, not where Christ was named, lest I should
build upon another man's foundation" (Rom. xv. 20). It
would be a plausible inference that the apostle is himself
regarded as the foundation of his mission churches (cp.
1 Cor. iii. 10). Christ is the foundation of the Church as a
whole, but within this community and walking in Christ's
steps, each apostle is in his own sphere a foundation stone
—an image which can be varied by calling the apostles

"pillars" (Gal. ii. 9). Further, the apostles share the function which ultimately belongs solely to God or to Christ, that of building the whole house or temple. St Paul sees himself as a fellow-worker with God on the building which God builds (1 Cor. iii. 9); hence the significance of the term "edification" in missionary vocabulary (*e.g.* 2 Cor. x. 8; cp. Eph. ii. 20 ff., iv. 12, 16).

Only once do the New Testament Epistles apply the metaphor of a shepherd to an apostle, and then only indirectly (1 Cor. ix. 7). He is described more explicitly as the gardener who plants a garden; thus St Paul can say, "I have planted, Apollos watered; but God gave the increase. . . . For we are labourers together with God: ye are God's husbandry" (1 Cor. iii. 6, 9). As usual, the apostle is the servant of God, and it is He who gives the increase; but a function has been entrusted to him which normally belongs to God or the Messiah, namely the planting of the vineyard and the care of the individual plants. The metaphor is then transferred to the ploughed field, where the apostle works as a sower—an image which is taken up by St Paul in yet another context (1 Cor. ix. 11). Finally, when Christ is the Bridegroom, the apostle can be depicted not only as the Bridegroom's friend (Mark ii. 19), but also as he who gives away the Bride, who has authority in his Lord's place even to ratify a betrothal. This is implicit in St Paul's statement that he has espoused the Church in Corinth to Christ, "that I may present you as a chaste virgin to Christ" (2 Cor. xi. 2).

The ministry of an apostle, then, is above all else an extension of Christ's own ministry and work. There is, of course, the fundamental difference that Christ's Messianic activity was unique, and therefore definitive; it included revelation, expiatory sacrifice, and victory over the powers of evil. But the work of Christ during His earthly life was in fact a divine redemptive activity within the Kingdom of God which was already established upon earth by virtue of the Incarnation. The work of the Risen Lord through His duly chosen and accredited representatives in the local churches which they founded and governed was a visible and authentic continuation of the same work of redemption which Christ began in Galilee. Naturally, the situation was changed, if we pay due regard to what happened between the Galilean ministry of Jesus and the Apostolic Age. The necessities of the local churches and of missionary work resulted in a differentiation of ministerial functions. All the more remarkable, therefore, is the continuity which still remained; and for this there is no other explanation than that the Kingdom of God before Christ's death, and the Church after His Resurrection, claimed the adherence and membership of men in the same interior and exterior ways. Regarded from this angle, the scope of the Ministry cannot be confined to the special function of the Apostolate. The Church continues to exist and to work, and the functions which were handed over by the Lord of the Church to the apostles are passed on by them to new officers. There is therefore no justification for making a radical division between the Apostolate and the local ministries, though we often find a demarcation of this kind in discussions of the organization of the Early Church. It is of course only reasonable that certain qualifications and tasks should be restricted to the apostles, giving them the special position which they undoubtedly have. They alone are eye-witnesses of the revelations of the Risen Lord, they are responsible for the expansion and organization of the Church, and they alone expound the original message of Jesus Christ. But the work of representing Christ in the Christian community, and of acting on His behalf, does not end here.

The impression which the New Testament gives of other ministries than the Apostolate is at first a confusing one. Their multiplicity, and the lack of a hierarchically graded organization, make it difficult to specify what missionary and ministerial offices existed or to define their nature. The pertinent question whether we ought to speak of a "ministry" at all during the earliest phase of the Church is, however, sufficiently answered by a reference to the Apostolate. No matter how we define this category of Christ's representatives, the apostles were unquestionably the sustaining, guiding and uniting element not only in the broad mission fields but also in the separate local churches. As long as the apostles lived, there was nothing to prevent tentative experiments with subordinate and more differentiated offices. It is significant that the actual terms describing the various offices cast little light on their function and scope.

It is not our intention to attempt the many questions connected with the different offices in Early Christianity. It may, however, be appropriate to turn once again to the metaphorical language of the New Testament, in order to show what the various ministers performed. We shall then find that the continuity in ministerial functions which we were able to establish between Christ and the apostles extends to elders and *episcopoi*. The apostles are called stewards in the household where God or Christ is envisaged as the master. This is also the case with the other officers. The Pastoral Epistles speak at length of "the house of God, which is the church of the living God"; the image then shifts to the building: "the pillar and ground of the truth" (1 Tim. iii. 15). The apostle exhorts his disciple to work among the servants of the House as "a good minister of Jesus Christ" (1 Tim. iv. 6), and to know "how thou oughest to behave thyself in the house of God" (*ibid*. iii. 15). Titus is urged to see that nothing is lacking to those who are entrusted to him; this, too, is the task of a steward (Tit. i. 5, iii. 13). The bishop "must be blameless, as the steward of God" (Tit. i. 7); the twice-described ideal of a head of a church (1 Tim. iii. 2 ff.; Tit. i. 7 ff.) is surely dependent upon the characterizations which Christ has given of faithful and unfaithful stewards (*e.g.* Luke xii. 42 ff.). The stewards who in the First Epistle of St Peter are exhorted to be "good stewards of the manifold grace of God" are, from the context, to be conceived primarily as ministers (1 Pet. iv. 10 f.). The elders of the churches addressed in the same Epistle are charged to "feed the flock of God" and to be "ensamples to the flock" (1 Pet. v. 2 f.). The shepherd must take care of the community at whose head he has been placed. Accord-

ing to Acts, St Paul gives the same injunction to those who
have charge of the Church in Ephesus: "Take heed therefore
unto yourselves, and to all the flock, over the which the Holy
Ghost hath made you overseers, to feed the church of God"
(xx. 28). These ministers are shepherds, because they
carry on in the Christian Church the work of Christ, the
Chief Shepherd (1 Pet. v. 4); for it is He who, through His
representatives, is still "the Shepherd and Bishop of your
souls" (*ibid.* ii. 25). The striking image of the husbandman,
applied to Timothy in one of the Pastoral Epistles (2 Tim.
ii. 6), can be explained as Pauline terminology: we have
already met it as applied to the Apostle himself (1 Cor.
ix. 7). The image of the pilot is once hinted at by St Paul,
though not in connection with a definite office (1 Cor. xii.
28), but it appears subsequently in the literature of the Early
Church, where it characterizes the function of the bishop.
The same is also true of the other metaphors; the steward,
the shepherd and the gardener are all among the metaphors
subsequently applied by ecclesiastical authors to illustrate
the nature of the mission and activities of the Christian
Ministry.

Up to this point our survey, and not least our examination
of the Biblical imagery, has aimed at demonstrating an
analogy between the Church and the Ministry. We have
arrived at an ever clearer view of the connection between the
eschatological community gathered around Jesus and the
Church which grew up after His Resurrection; and in the
same way we can assert an identity and continuity between
Christ's own ministry and the ministries which are performed
after Him by persons appointed in the Church. There is
identity because Christ's Ministry is composite, and embraces
all the ecclesiastical ministries which are undertaken on His
behalf and in His name. Continuity is clear from the fact
that the ministers fill the same functions in the Church that
Christ ministerially performed during His life on earth.
Just as His Ministry took human form because He was
incarnate, it will henceforth be committed to and discharged
by men who are invested with His authority and act as His

representatives. The visible nature of the Ministry is thus congruous with the Incarnation. Christ's own Ministry determined the beginnings of the Christian Church, as they took shape during His lifetime. In the same way, the Ministry is an integral part of the Church in the period between the Resurrection and the Second Coming; it performs vital functions in the life of the Christian community.

If, in considering the character of the Ministry, we tried to draw a hard-and-fast line between Christ and His apostles, or between the apostles and the other officers, we should be forced to assume fundamental differences in the function and structure of the Church during different eras. The question is this: Is there room to suppose that the ways in which men encountered and were called into the Kingdom of Heaven on earth were essentially different in Christ's time, in the days of the apostles, and again during subsequent centuries? Our instinctive answer must surely be that they were not. Quite the contrary; we see in the continuity of the Ministry an indication that the function and ministrations of the Church will never change from the time of Christ's earthly life until He who is now Invisible has come again in His glory.

The purpose of the Ministry is to represent in a twofold way. We have been dealing mainly with the minister as a plenipotentiary, acting on Christ's commission and in His name. And, indeed, this is his most characteristic function; it amounts in the end to a manifestation of divine truth and of the power of the Kingdom of God, analogous to the calling of the incarnate Christ to be the "brightness of God's glory and the express image of his person" (Heb. i. 3). But besides this, the minister is also the representative of man. In this capacity, he gathers in one person the multiplicity of individuals and, in the higher grades of the ministry, of churches into a single unity, and presents to God the sum of their worship and supplications.

The function of the Ministry is most plainly seen when the Christian community takes visible form at Divine Service. The structure of the Church is then revealed in the liturgical action of minister and congregation. At the same time, it becomes easier to understand what is meant by representation. The minister assumes the part of Christ, and the congregation is the People of God; the model is first that of Christ surrounded by the community which He assembled around Him, and secondly, always very real to the first Christians, that of the glorified Christ and the heavenly congregation gathered for worship about God's throne. The realization that worship on earth is a reflection of the celestial worship underlies both the Epistle to the Hebrews and the Revelation. It is therefore perfectly consonant with Christianity to think that, in the discharge of his office, the leader of the service reflects both Christ in the circle of His own, and Christ the Heavenly High Priest. He stands in Christ's place for all to see when, in the rite which is expressive of all Christian life and worship, he blesses the bread and the wine: "This is my Body . . . This is my Blood of the new testament . . ." A consideration too often ignored is that we could not imagine any form of breaking of bread or of making Eucharist in the early Church, even at the earliest stages of the rite, without some person to bless the food in the words uttered by Christ at His Last Supper, and to act as Christ acted. This we can definitely affirm, because Christ's words and actions at the Supper follow the usage of the Jewish householder at ceremonial meals, not least in connection with the eating of the paschal lamb. Therefore, particularly during the first centuries of the Church, the image of the household must have been present to the congregation at the Eucharist, and at every such meeting one person must have functioned as the master of the house. As, at the same time, it was always a *sacrament*, the presiding person performed his duties on behalf of Christ. This means that in the Church it is from the Ministry as representative of Christ that the real nature of Divine Service has from the beginning been derived. We may appropriately refer here to the words which have been handed down by St Luke and St Paul in connection with the institution of the Eucharist: "This do in remembrance of me" (Luke xxii. 19; 1 Cor. xi. 24 f.). The very structure of the Supper entitles us to interpret the words as addressed not only to the Christian community in general, but to the disciples in particular, since they were intended to represent Christ presiding at the meal which was to be the most intimate and characteristic activity of the Church. It is probably from the Eucharist that other forms of Christian worship derived their character. As preacher, teacher and pastor, the minister is a Christ to his congregation; and on the other hand, he is the mouthpiece of his congregation in thanksgiving and prayer before Christ and His Father.

It is therefore surely no accident that, in the exhaustive treatment which he gives to public worship and the life of the Christian community in his First Epistle to the Corinthians (x–xiv), St Paul discusses what we can call "the hier-archy of representation". The introduction shows that the author considers the matter to be important: "But *I would have you know* that the head of every man is Christ; and the head of the woman is the man; and the head of Christ is God" (*ibid*. xi. 3). The whole of this section (xi. 3–16), con-taining arguments which may be hard to follow or accept, especially in modern times, deals with an order created by God to prevail wherever He works among men. One of its themes is that the central links in the sequence "God – Christ—the man—the woman" are charged with represent-ing those which are superior to those which are inferior. This idea is expressed more clearly in the word "image", which also occurs a little further on: "For a man indeed ought not to cover his head, forasmuch as he is the image and glory of God" (xi. 7). Now Christ, as we know, became flesh to represent and reveal God to mankind; thus we read of Him "who is the image of the invisible God" (Col. i. 15) and of "the glorious gospel of Christ, who is the image of God" (2 Cor. iv. 4; cp. Heb. i. 3). The same applies to the man in this sequence. When he is described first as God's image and glory, and then as the head of the woman, it is because he in his own created person has to reflect and reveal God and Christ to the woman and to the whole of creation. This specifically New Testament line of thought comes out still more plainly in the so-called domestic codes, particularly in the Epistle to the Ephesians: "For the husband is the head of the wife, even as Christ is the head of the church . . ." (Eph. v. 23 ff.). It should be stressed that the books of the New Testament are far from making any absolute assessment in this order of functions; on the contrary, it is emphatically stated that man and woman have been created for one another, that they are dependent on one another, and have to serve each in his own way. "Nevertheless, neither is the man without the woman, neither the woman without the man, in the Lord. For as the woman is of the man, even so is the man also by the woman; but all things of God" (1 Cor. xi. 11 f.). The Christian estimate of human worth and of the possibility of salvation is expressed by St Paul in his Epistle to the Galatians: "There is neither Jew nor Greek, there is neither bond nor free, there is neither male nor female: for ye are all one in Christ Jesus" (iii. 28). This attitude is especially clear with regard to the sacrament of baptism. The, in our eyes, surprising assignment to the two sexes of different functions in the hierarchy of representation is due to the clear awareness of early Christianity that man and woman were created by God to represent in their own relations to one another the relationship between Christ and the Church. Therefore the domestic code of the Epistle to the Ephesians ends with the words: "This is a great mystery; but I say that it concerns Christ and the church" (v. 32). The order of creation and the order of salvation thus correspond at that point.

Against this background, then, we have to place the representation of Christ which is characteristic of Christian worship, and also of the Ministry in all its functions. Inasmuch as the man, as a householder, reflects Christ in His relations to the Church-Bride and to the congregation-household, it must have seemed self-evident to the Early Christian mind that the officer presiding over the assembled congregation, and therefore at the Eucharist, should be a male. Even without this, ministerial duties as outlined in

the New Testament could to a great extent be called mascu-
line, particularly as regards authoritative governing and
judicial functions. These, after all, are where the ministers
act on Christ's behalf, and it is in full conformity with the
idea of representation that the officers who founded churches
and led congregations were men. Thus it is no mere chance
that we find in the New Testament unanimous pronouncements as to the different functions of the two sexes, and can
establish that the ministers of the Church were invariably
men, namely, the apostles sent forth with full authority by
Christ, the missionaries who founded churches, and the
heads of the local congregations. It is unlikely that the
absence of female ministers should be due to any consideration paid by Christ and the early Church to the socially
inferior position of the woman at that time. For one thing,
there were priestesses in a number of Hellenistic cults; for
another, Christianity was from the start no stranger to
radical reassessments, including those of a social nature, and
not least as regards women's status in marriage and their
equal worth as human beings. And the final, most important point to bear in mind is that the call to work in the
community is by no means reserved solely for the special
officers of the Church.

Our aim has been to show how the Ministry is part of the
structure of the Church in the same way as the Messiah is
indivisibly united to the structure of the People of God.
With the help of those who speak and act in His name,
Christ as the Glorified Lord continues in His Church the
work among mankind which He performed in word and deed
during His life on earth. Though invisible, He thus still
works in a visible and personal way through the Ministry
which represents Him and, through His power, brings the
gifts of salvation within the reach of mankind.

VII

A SYNOPSIS OF EARLY CHRISTIAN PREACHING

Bo Reicke

I. INTRODUCTION

WHEN SENDING out His twelve Apostles to the lost sheep of the chosen people, our Lord commanded them to *preach* (Matt. x. 7; Mark iii. 14; Luke ix. 2). There are no specimens of this preliminary Christian preaching, and yet there is every reason to believe that it really took place. But how at this early stage could the Apostles know what to say, and how could they prepare their speeches without any rhetorical training? According to Matthew x. 19 the Holy Ghost would teach them what to say later, when they appeared before governors and judges, so that they need not worry about rhetorical preparation. Many scholars have assumed that this pneumatic spontaneity was generally characteristic of the earliest preaching of the Gospel.[1] However, since form criticism has revealed the pre-literary forms of popular tradition, it seems impossible any longer to suppose that the earliest Christian preaching was without set forms. Researches in comparative folklore also suggest that no stage of cultural development was ever entirely without traditional forms. Moreover, the specimens of the earliest apostolic preaching after Christ's resurrection, as given in Acts, are clearly formed on a common pattern.[2] Because of their primitive Christology (*e.g.* Jesus is called *pais*), it is reasonable to look upon these speeches as con-

---

[1] For instance M. Schian, "Geschichte der christlichen Predigt", *Realencykl. für prot. Theol. und Kirche* (3rd ed.) xv. (1904), p. 628 f.
[2] E. Norden, *Agnostos Theos* (1913), p. 8 ff.; M. Dibelius, *Formgeschichte des Evangeliums* (2nd ed. 1930), p. 15 ff.

forming to a real tradition,[1] and not as later constructions of Luke.

This makes it necessary to presuppose the existence of more or less elaborate forms of apostolic preaching soon after the resurrection of Christ, if not already in His lifetime. Although the apostolic message was something quite new and *sui generis*, we must also look for the causes and origins of its forms; for historical research does not indicate any creation *ex nihilo* of external forms. So we must ask the question: Whence did the Apostles derive the forms of their early preaching?

In answer to this question it is first of all necessary to refer to the teaching of Jesus. Perhaps there were also influences from outside; but literary evidence for such influences at an early stage is weak and has little weight, since the disciples received daily instruction from the Lord Himself. As to the forms of the Master's own preaching, He was probably indebted to Old Testament prophecies as well as to such messianic proclamations as those in the *Book of Enoch* or the *Testaments of the Twelve Patriarchs*. But the preaching of the first Apostles must principally have depended upon the personal teaching of Jesus. Indirectly this is also true of Christian preaching in later apostolic times. One fact is of extraordinary importance: the Apostles were the representatives of the Lord, and an extension or multiplication of His person (Matt. x. 1 ff., etc.).

To understand the principal forms of apostolic preaching there are, accordingly, reasons for comparing the apostolic traditions with the sayings of Jesus in the Gospels. This does not mean that the Apostles always repeated in their preaching what the Lord had said. It means that when they were sent out to preach, they had to perform an activity which ought as far as possible to correspond to what Jesus had Himself performed as the Messenger of God. And this activity must be studied from different aspects, because the

---

[1] Dibelius, p. 16. He further compares the kerygma in the sermons of Acts with the kerygma in Paul's epistles. On p. 20 he concludes: "Eine solche Art der Traditionsfortpflanzung entspricht offenbar dem Brauch im palästinischen wie im hellenistischen Judentum."

relations between the preacher and the hearers might differ.

Different Aspects of a Divine Messenger's Activity

The first duty of a divine messenger, in the Old as well as in the New Testament, was to convert his disobedient contemporaries. In fulfilling this task he was intended to preach in another way than when he addressed believers. Thus (1) *"conversion"* may be considered a primary purpose of a messenger's activity. It has immediately to be divided into two parts: *"admonition"* and *"invitation"*. *"Admonition"*, or the reproof of existing wickedness, was a specially important task of the Old Testament prophets. In succession to them, John the Baptist was the first to preach admonition in New Testament times; sometimes Jesus and the Apostles also admonished people, although the condemnatory aspect was not very prominent in the primitive Gospel. *"Invitation"* was considerably more important to the New Testament preachers. Jesus generously invited people to enter the Kingdom, while the Apostles and Christian missionaries invited them to enter the Church. The latter form of invitation did not claim to be anything but a continuation of the former. A similar correspondence between Jesus and the Apostles may also be claimed for their communication of (2) *"instruction"* and *"edification"* to disciples already won. The apostolic exhortation and advice to the churches, of which the New Testament epistles give examples, were certainly meant to be a continuation of such instructions of the Master as are represented, for example, in Matthew v–vii or xviii. Thus (1) *conversion*, including admonition and invitation, and (2) *instruction* and *edification*, were the most important functions of a divine messenger in the New Testament world.

But there were also two quite special forms of instruction which may in practice be treated as independent aspects of preaching. They are properly to be considered in connection with Jesus, but partly also in connection with His followers.

(3) Having performed His work among men, Christ bade farewell to the Twelve, gave them His last charge, and renewed the covenant with them in the Eucharist and His subsequent death. In these events a unique action was performed by the Saviour because a new relation was created between Him and the disciples; the words which He then pronounced are not simply to be identified with His general instruction. In making this distinction, support may be found in Jewish traditions of the Patriarchs who gave formal farewell discourses as in Genesis xlix and similar passages. There was, in fact, a definite convention governing testamentary discourses. Our Lord's farewell speeches belong to this form of tradition.[1] Because the texts in question all have as their subject-matter a divine mediator's departure and last will, we may conveniently classify them under the title of "*testament*". The testament form has also survived to some extent in the apostolic literature. Finally, there are (4) sayings referring to the messenger's experiences of the other world. In so far as these sayings took the form of real speeches, they may be included under the heading of "*revelation*".

It is hoped that the expressions used here, (1) *conversion*, including admonition and invitation, (2) *instruction* and *edification*, (3) *testament* and (4) *revelation*, will serve to characterize the main aspects of a Biblical messenger's activity, whether we are discussing the Patriarchs and the Prophets, or Jesus and the Apostles, or their successors. A classification of New Testament preaching in terms of these functions of a preacher seems to be most useful for a detailed understanding of the relationship between Jesus as the supreme Messenger and His immediate followers.

Different Kinds of Preacher

The Apostles were partly missionaries or evangelists, and partly ruling authorities in churches already established.

---

[1] J. Munck, "Discours d'adieu dans le Nouveau Testament et dans la littérature biblique", *Aux sources de la tradition chrétienne*. *Mélanges offerts à Maurice Goguel* (1950), pp. 155–170.

In the former capacity they spoke in terms of admonition and invitation; the other aspects of their preaching were more closely connected with the second capacity. Yet in both capacities it was properly in succession to the Lord Himself that they preached. This is also true of their personal disciples. All these teachers claimed to reproduce the words of the Lord.

In addition to (a) Jesus and (b) the Apostles and evangelists it is further necessary to take into account as preachers in the Early Church (c) the ordinary ministers and laymen in the local congregations. There is extant no literary evidence for this congregational preaching, but there is indirect evidence for it in the New Testament epistles, and even the epistles themselves may reveal something about congregational preaching when they record such apostolic sayings as "Timothy . . . who shall bring you into remembrance of my ways in Christ Jesus, as I teach everywhere in every congregation" (1 Cor. iv. 17); or "These things shall you command and teach" (1 Tim. iv. 11). The expositions given in the epistles were to be models for congregational instruction and preaching. Although the congregational preachers had scarcely themselves formed part of the Lord's own audience, the personal and literary oversight of the Apostles and their colleagues clearly replaced the Lord's own oral teaching as the means by which congruity was maintained between congregational preaching in the churches and the mind of Jesus. This at least was how the Early Church understood the matter.[1]

II. CLASSIFICATION ACCORDING TO FORMS OF PREACHING AND KINDS OF PREACHER

We have tried to distinguish four aspects of the Master's preaching: (1) conversion, including admonition and invitation; (2) instruction and edification; (3) testament;

[1] N. A. Dahl, "Anamnesis", *Studia theol.*, 1, 1948, p. 74 ff.

(4) revelation; and three kinds of preacher: (a) Jesus; (b) the Apostles and others, acting as evangelists or as rulers; (c) congregational ministers and laymen in the rôle of preachers. Our thesis is now that the secondary messengers, kinds (b) and (c), adopted methods corresponding to the various forms of preaching used by Jesus as the Divine Messenger *par excellence*.

This attempt at classification is partly based upon theoretical considerations, as is inevitable since sources for the study of early Christian preaching are few. It may not be possible to exemplify all the forms of preaching in each case. Yet such a systematic classification will be valuable if it helps towards a better understanding, and if it can be legitimately made in a subject which must otherwise remain obscure and vague. It must also be admitted that there are no clear-cut distinctions between the different categories here employed. The different forms of preaching will sometimes overlap, for instance when instruction and edification prove to contain the same message or kerygma as invitation. Nevertheless, the classification proposed may be valuable in practise.

It is further to be remarked that a sermon need not necessarily be part of a formal service in order to be regarded as preaching.[1] All speeches which can be regarded as examples of preaching were "cultic" because they had to do with the service of God, but this does not mean they were always themselves parts of a ritual ceremony. The free speeches of the Christian missionaries must also be studied as forms of preaching although they had no context in formal divine worship. On the other hand, liturgy influenced the preaching of the Church, directly and indirectly,[2] just as Old Testament prophecy was probably influenced by liturgical forms.[3]

---

[1] Schian, *op. cit.*, p. 628.
[2] Y. Brilioth, *Predikans historia* (1945), p. 10 f.
[3] A cultic view of the Prophets is specially emphasized by Scandinavian interpreters such as S. Mowinckel, *Psalmenstudien*, iii. (1923), p. 4 ff.; A. Haldar, *Associations of Cult Prophets among the Ancient Semites* (1945), p. 92 ff.; I. Engnell, "Profetia och tradition", *Svensk exegetisk årsbok*, 13 (1947), p. 114 ff.

(1) *Conversion, including Admonition and Invitation*

Admonition.—The Mosaic and prophetic discourses of the Old Testament are concerned with judgment as well as salvation. Of these subjects judgment is the more conspicuous. In later Christian preaching judgment was often a very important subject; but this is really an Old Testament emphasis, for the preacher must not forget to preach the Law. In the New Testament admonitory sermons are much less frequent than comforting discourses. Yet there are instances of sermons containing reproof in the New Testament, first in connection with John the Baptist (Matt. iii. 7–10) and then in connection with Jesus and the Apostles.

(*a*) Jesus began His preaching with an exhortation to repent, before He made His generous invitation to enter the Kingdom (Matt. iv. 17 ff.). It is to be regretted that the Synoptic Gospels have not reported any admonitory sermon at this point. On the other hand, they contain several illustrations of how Jesus opposed unbelievers, Pharisees and the Jewish hierarchy. These examples will serve as illustrations of the admonitory speeches delivered by Jesus. The Gospel of John especially gives information on this matter. Already in John ii. 16 f. an anti-Jewish discourse is reported (after the cleansing of the Temple), and similar discourses are found in abbreviated forms throughout the same Gospel (*e.g.* viii. 34 ff.). In the Synoptic Gospels the woes against the rich and against the cities of Galilee, the Beelzebub controversy and the great anti-pharisaic speech, are the most considerable instances (Luke vi. 24–26; Matt. xi. 20–24, xii. 25–37, xiii. 1–36 and their parallels). But it must be noticed that Jesus did not, like the Prophets, rebuke contemporary life indiscriminately. Only when it was disobedient to His message did He call it an evil and adulterous generation or the like (Matt. xii. 39 ff.; cf. Matt. xi. 16 ff., xii. 45 and their parallels, xvii. 17, xxiii. 29 ff.; Mark viii. 38). All these passages belong to proclamations which, in their present form, seem to be abstracts of longer speeches.

(*b*) The Apostles and their successors being evangelists, were also rather cautious in assuming admonitory rôles in their missionary preaching. In principle they seem to have started with a direct invitation to salvation, which is more fully treated below. But in Romans i. 18–iii. 20 there is a long section on the wickedness of men, Gentiles as well as Jews, and it is scarcely possible to avoid the impression that here, Paul has reproduced such discourses as he and his colleagues used to give when publicly attacking Jews and Gentiles in order to convince them of the necessity of conversion. He has probably given the readers a specimen of this preaching, starting from the declaration in i. 16 that he is not ashamed of the Gospel. In doing so he changed the presentation from a direct address to an objective description, but there are still features of a personal address left when the second person and the vocative are used in ii. 1, 3–5, 17, 27. Compare the doxologies and other traces of rhetorical style. The usages of oral speech are found here as well as later on, although later Paul did not keep so closely to the preaching form as in the first section. Thus at least in Romans i. 18–iii. 20 an indirect specimen of apostolic admonitory preaching can be seen. Evidence of similar polemic activity is given in 2 Corinthians x. 3–6, where Paul certainly speaks of unbelievers as well as of seduced believers, stating that he can defeat everything that exalts itself against the knowledge of God, and that his weapons are not carnal. It is also probable that the Apostles in general tried in this way to fulfil the Lord's prophecy in John xvi. 8 of the coming of the Paraclete, "he will reprove the world of sin", although there are hardly any other examples of such preaching.

When believers are criticized in the apostolic writings for wrong ideas and conduct, there is no admonition (in the present sense) but instruction (which is treated below); admonition is properly addressed to unbelievers in order to move them to repentance. This does not mean that the same speeches of rebuke were never used to stir up the repentance of believers already converted, as is illustrated by Romans i–iii, where Christian readers are made to reflect anew on the general wickedness of man. Such use of material intended to stimulate conversion is also important in later Christian preaching (when the minister is preaching "the Law"). It may look like a paradox, yet, in this secondary connection, it is possible to speak of the admonition of Christians. But it is really a secondary form of admonition, a return to "The first principles of the words of God" (Heb. v. 12).

(c) Admonition of unbelievers was certainly also practised by ministers and laymen in the congregations, although there is no literary evidence of such preaching. There are only such hints of it as in 1 Corinthians xiv. 24, where an unbeliever is said to enter a Christian congregation and be convicted and judged by everybody's "prophesying", which seems to mean preaching after the fashion of the prophets, or admonition. Furthermore, the apostolic writers were not very satisfied with the general standard of zeal in this matter, but felt obliged to remind their readers of their duty to behave charitably (e.g. Col. iii. 8 ff.; 2 Tim. ii. 23 ff.; 1 Pet. ii. 1, and especially Jas. i. 19 ff., iii. 1 ff.).

In New Testament religion, admonition usually stands in close relation to invitation and has value only as a background to it. Conversion is the end to which both are subordinated.

Invitation.—The essential purpose of New Testament preaching was invitation, and indeed invitation to something that was already known to be proleptically present. The Old Testament preaching of the glory to come was thus transformed,[1] as was the Baptist's messianic preaching (Matt. iii. 11 f. and parallels).

(a) In Galilee, Jesus connected His initial exhortation to repent with an immediate announcement of the Gospel (Mark i. 15). According to the Synoptists He did not proclaim Himself publicly as the Messiah; this had provisionally to be a secret. He called disciples, however, and performed signs and miracles by which it was possible to understand that He was the Holy One of God (Mark i. 24 and parallel). So when the Synoptists say that Jesus preached

---

[1] G. Wingren, *Predikan* (1949), p. 57.

in the synagogues (Matt. iv. 23, etc.), with a quite special power (Mark i. 22, 27 and parallel), it is natural to see in this preaching a concealed invitation to belief in Himself. Luke has illustrated how Jesus applied Old Testament prophecies to His own person (iv. 16–30). To those who had ears to hear it was already a divine kerygma, like the later apostolic kerygma, with the one difference that what He had told them in darkness they should afterwards speak in light (Matt. x. 27).

As is well known, no explicit autokerygma of Jesus is found in the Synoptic Gospels outside Matthew xi. 25–30, whereas it is more frequent in the Gospel of John. The first outsiders in this Gospel to receive information as to His real nature are Nicodemus and the woman of Samaria (John iii. 13 ff., iv. 13 ff.). There follow many similar examples of autokerygma, some even more explicit, in particular when He proclaims Himself with the words "I am", etc. All these quotations seem to be fragments of longer speeches or sermons, changed into dialogues to gain dramatic power. They are either real reports of the Lord's preaching, as far as this was known to the Evangelist, or instances of the sort of preaching that was current in the Evangelist's church, the ordinary form of proclamation "He is" having in the latter case been changed into "I am". Perhaps both possibilities can be granted. In any case there is reason to suppose a connection between the preaching of the Church and the sayings of Jesus as reproduced in the Gospel.[1]

Here it may be remarked that Christ's teachings about Himself have their background not only in the Old Testament messianic prophecies and psalms, but also in the Wisdom literature (cp. Matt. xi. 28–30 with Ecclus. xxiv., li. 23 ff.,[2] and the *Odes of Solomon*, xxxiii).[3] But Jewish beliefs about Wisdom were of international currency. This may

---

[1] For the Synoptic Gospels, see M. Dibelius, *Formgeschichte des Evangeliums*, p. 25 ff., 234 ff.; for John, see A. Fridrichsen, *Johannesevangeliet* (1939), p. 35 f., 55 f.

[2] T. Arvedson, *Das Mysterium Christi. Eine Studie zu Mt* 11. 25–30 (1937), p. 10 ff., 94, 180 ff.

[3] Arvedson, p. 170 ff.

help us to explain the striking resemblance of some New Testament passages to such proclamations as are found in the *Corpus Hermeticum* (i. 27 ff., iv. 4, etc.).[1]

Further, it is remarkable that the Synoptists often connect the Master's secret kerygma with synagogue worship. This corresponds to the practice of the Apostles as described in Acts, which is also evidence of the relations to be inferred between the Master's kerygma and that of the Apostles. When the Lord preached in a synagogue (Luke iv. 16–30), He used Holy Scripture as the text for His own messianic announcement. This method was adopted by the Apostles when they preached sermons to prove Jesus to be the Elect One. It is probable that Jesus had often explained the Scriptures to His disciples privately in order to teach their fulfilment in His Person, although there is no direct evidence for this in His lifetime. But from the days after His resurrection there are indications of such teaching; compare the Emmaus appearance according to Luke xxiv. 27: "beginning at Moses and all the prophets, He expounded unto them in all the Scriptures the things concerning Himself", and His subsequent appearance in Jerusalem according to Luke xxiv. 44–49, where the elements of the later apostolic kerygma are already present. These appearances of the Risen Christ may very well be connected with foreshadowings given in His earthly life. We may also compare the predictions of the Passion in Matthew xvi. 21 ff., etc.

(*b*) The missionary or conversion sermons of the Apostles may similarly have developed themes given by the Master. When studying these sermons it is relevant to observe that they closely conform to a logical scheme which is typical of arguments designed to persuade, namely (1) thesis, (2) proofs, (3) conclusion. Topics of early apostolic preaching that were already provided by Jesus are the following: (1) The central thesis of the kerygma, that He was the Servant and the Lord; and two of the main proofs of it, namely (2*a*) that His life showed Him to fulfil these titles, and (2*b*) that the

---

[1] Quoted by G. Friedrich, *kēryssō*, *Theol. Wörterb. zum N.T.*, iii. (1938), p. 697.

Holy Scriptures bore witness to Him. There were two further and novel proofs of His Messiahship: (2c) the established fact of His resurrection, and (2d) the miracles which showed the power of His risen life. Finally (3) the conclusion was reached in consequence of these weighty arguments, that everybody must turn to the Lord, including the Gentiles. These are the standard topics of the early missionary sermons as they were related in Acts. More precisely the conversion sermons of Acts, at least those preached to Jews, contain the following standard series of items:—

(1) Thesis: the kerygma of Jesus as the Elect One of God, the Suffering Servant and the Risen Lord.

(2) Proofs:

> (a) the Jews were eye-witnesses of His miracles and mercy, His humiliation and execution, which proves that He was the Servant [1];
>
> (b) the Scriptures foretold His resurrection as well as other events of His life;
>
> (c) the Apostles bore witness to His resurrection, which proves that He is the Lord;
>
> (d) His present power and miracles, and the gift of the Holy Ghost, prove His continuing activity in the Church.

(3) Conclusion: the need for both Jews and Gentiles to repent and to be baptized.[2]

All these items are not always present, and they do not appear strictly in the order given above. Even the kerygma itself is sometimes only implied. But all the sermons in question can validly be regarded as variations of this general pattern. Consider the first sermon in Acts, the Pentecostal

---

[1] They saw but did not understand. On the question whether the Church was right in representing Jesus as the Suffering Servant, see a brilliant discussion in J. W. Bowman, *The Intention of Jesus* (1945), p. 41 ff.

[2] A standard pattern, but with another classification, may be studied in M. Dibelius, *Formgeschichte*, p. 15; cf. C. H. Dodd, *The Apostolic Preaching and Its Developments* (new impr. 1949), p. 21 ff.; R. Leijs, "Prédication des Apôtres", *Nouv. rev. théol.*, lxxix. (1947), p. 607; B. Gärtner, "Missionspredikan i Apostla-gärningarna", *Svensk exeg. årsb.*, 15 (1950), p. 36 ff.

speech of Peter (ii. 22–39), disregarding its exordium on the prophecy of Joel. Point (1), the kerygma, does not appear first as for example in v. 31, but after the various arguments of point (2), that is, in ii. 36. Otherwise the sermon conforms to the schedule; (2a) appears in verse 22 f., (2b) in 24–31, (2c) in 32 and (2d) in 33 ff.; then, after the kerygma in 36, comes (3), the conclusion, in 38 f. The arrangement of the first speech of Paul reported in Acts xiii. 16–41 is similar. After an exordium on the history of Israel, the kerygma or point (1) is presented in verses 24–26; then the arguments follow in this order: (2a) in 27 f., (2b) in 29, 32–37, (2c) in 30 f.—(2d) is missing; and finally there is the conclusion, point (3), in verses 38–41 (cp. 46 f.). There is thus a close parallel between the first sermons of the two greatest Apostles, obviously based on a fixed pattern. By this arrangement Luke endeavoured to give representative examples of the missionary preaching of the two leading Apostles,[1] inserting them at the beginning of his two main sections which are concerned with Peter and Paul respectively. These reproductions are probably reliable, as they are meant to be typical examples of their conversion preaching. It is unlikely that they are free compositions of the author because they betray traces of a peculiar christology. As Jesus of Nazareth is described as the Servant here only, and not in other parts of Acts except iv. 27, 30 and viii. 32–35, it seems wrong to consider them an invention of Luke. A far more probable hypothesis is that these speeches preserve early traditions. The slight differences between them are added evidence for their authenticity. Thus there are reasons for assuming that the speeches in Acts are good evidence for the way in which the apostles preached.[2] The other sermons of

---

[1] H. J. Cadbury, "The Speeches in Acts", *The Beginnings of Christianity*, v. (1933), p. 425; O. Bauernfeind, *Die Apostelgeschichte* (1939), pp. 62–71; F. C. Bruce, *The Speeches in the Acts of the Apostles*, Tyndale New Testament Lecture, 1942 (1945) (not available to us); M. Dibelius, *Die Reden der Apostelgeschichte und die antike Geschichtsschreibung* (1949), p. 12 ff.

[2] This is also the opinion of Cadbury (p. 426 f.), in spite of his scepticism with regard to the arguments quoted above on the Christology and the formal variations (as to the *pais* Christology, cf. *idem*, "The Titles of Jesus in Acts", *ibid.*, p. 364 ff.). Dodd (p. 18 ff.) is less sceptical.

Peter, appearing in Acts iii. 12–26, v. 29–32, x. 34–43, are shorter than his Pentecost sermon but contain traces of the same principal ideas, though in somewhat varying forms. Point (1) appears in iii. 13, v. 30a, x. 36, 42; (2a) in iii. 14, v. 30b, x. 37–40; (2b) in iii. 18, 21 ff. (there is a short allusion to it in v. 30), x. 43a; (2c) in iii. 15, v. 31a, 32a, x. 40 f.; (2d) in iii. 12, 16, v. 32b (in x. 44 the Holy Ghost, not mentioned in the sermon, appears in the context); and finally, point (3) in iii. 17, 19, v. 31b, x. 43b. In spite of all variation there is a conservatism of form which is evidence for a living tradition. Presumably this tradition was kept alive not least because of its connection with baptism, as is evident from Acts ii. 38, 41, x. 47, 48. Luke certainly had recourse to current baptismal traditions when reconstructing the sermons.

The sermons we have considered are sermons before Jews. It may be added that when Paul delivered the great sermon reported in Acts xiii. 16 ff. to Jews in the synagogue at Pisidian Antioch, he spoke after the official reading of the Law and the Prophets, as Jesus did in Nazareth according to Luke iv. 16 ff. Compare also Philip and the information he gave to the eunuch who read Isaiah in Acts viii. 27 ff. However, even if these sermons were based upon a scriptural passage, they are not to be called "analytic", to use a homiletic term. Analytic sermons, such as the homilies of Origen, were a later production of the Church although they had an early background in Jewish literature; they were addressed to believers instructed in the Holy Scriptures as the accepted source of Christian belief, and this was not the situation when early Christians preached in the synagogue. Thus the sermons referred to are all "thematic", their subject being the kerygma.

There are two further sermons in Acts, which Paul is said to have delivered before heathen audiences: those at Lystra (xiv. 15–17), and at Athens (xvii. 22–31). It is obvious that both speeches are generally similar, though in the latter an abridgment of the Christian kerygma has been included in the exposition (xvii. 31). Reducing both speeches to their fundamental ideas one will get the following scheme:—

(1) Arguments:

> (a) the true God is the Creator of everything, and does not require such material sacrifices as are made by idolaters (xiv. 15c, xvii. 24 f.);
>
> (b) He has revealed Himself in nature as well as through human agencies, so that everybody ought to know Him (xiv. 17, xvii. 26 f.);
>
> (c) man feels kinship with the true God which should raise him above any materialist idolatry (xvii. 22 f., 27–29);
>
> (d) if God has so far been tolerant (xiv. 16, xvii. 30a), He has now proclaimed His will, and fixed a day of general trial before an elect Man, the proof being the latter's resurrection from the dead (xvii. 30b–31).

(2) Conclusion: it is necessary to be converted (xiv. 15b, xvii. 30b).

It is not easy to answer the question whether this correspondence means that Luke reproduced actual traditions of Pauline speeches, or that he inserted a general pattern that was perhaps known to him from Hellenistic literature.[1] Certainly it is possible to compare some items of these speeches with the epistles of Paul. For instance, Acts xiv. 17 may be compared with Romans i. 20, and Acts xvii. 25–29 with Romans i. 23–25. Nothing contradicts the assumption that Paul himself adopted such Hellenistic ideas, if they can indeed be shown to antedate him.[2] There are also similar adaptations of Greek forms in Hellenistic-Jewish literature. The most probable theory seems to be that Paul

---

[1] E. Norden, *Agnostos Theos*, p. 125; M. Dibelius, *Paulus auf dem Areopag* (1939), pp. 31, 39; M. Pohlenz, "Paulus und die Stoa", *Zeitschr. f. d. neutest. Wiss.*, xlii. (1949), pp. 69–98.

[2] Norden, *op. cit.*, p. 139 f.; A. Wikenhauser, *Die Apostelgeschichte und ihr Geschichtswert* (1921), p. 154; W. Schmid, "Die Rede des Apostels Paulus vor den Philosophen und Areopagiten in Athen", *Philologus*, xcv. (1942–43), p. 115 f.

was inspired by Hellenistic-Jewish literature to speak to the Gentiles in the way that Luke has described. Now this does not prove the complete historical authenticity of the tradition. The speeches, however, are probably examples of a Christian type, and not merely importations from Hellenism. It seems possible to test this assumption by a comparison with the *Kerygma Petri* [1] which is thought to be an Egyptian sermon from the first third of the second century.[2] In the short fragments of this sermon there are still clear echoes of the principal ideas expressed in Acts xiv. 15–17, xvii. 22–31. There is no question of direct dependence, and this may indicate the existence of an old Christian tradition of such preaching to the Gentiles.

In conclusion it may be stated that Acts give us a fairly good idea of apostolic conversion preaching to Jews as well as to Greeks.

(*c*) The task of inviting conversion was certainly performed by ordinary ministers and laymen within the congregations, but we cannot expect to find any literary evidence of such preaching. There are only hints of it in 1 Corinthians xiv. 24 f. For if the prophesying mentioned in this passage could lead to the conversion of outsiders, it may have included not only admonition, as was formerly pointed out, but also invitation. It is probable that this enthusiastic prophesying was a crude copy of the pneumatic sermons of the Apostles (cp. 1 Thess. i. 6–8, "ye became followers of us . . .").

(2) *Instruction and Edification*

In later preaching there is often no absolute difference between material intended for the conversion of outsiders and for the instruction of people already converted; the latter are also to remember their conversion, to recall the admonition delivered against their sins and to be thankful

---

[1] E. v. Dobschütz, *Das Kerygma Petri* (1893); Gärtner, p. 54.
[2] E. Hennecke, *Neutestamentliche Apokryphen* (2nd ed., 1924), p. 144 f.

for the divine grace communicated to them at their baptism.[1]
These various forms of preaching are necessary because man
is still living in the flesh. They also have New Testament
authority, as has already been noticed. Repetition of conversion motifs occurs, for instance, in Romans i–ii, vi;
1 Corinthians i. 26 ff., xv. 1–11 (summary of the kerygma);
Ephesians i. 3 ff.; Titus i. 11 ff. But even if the same themes
appear in both kinds of preaching, instruction is nevertheless
a form which demands independent treatment. For instruction, or the exhortation and advice given to believers, is
peculiarly adapted to the internal needs of the Christian
community. Later, when it took the form of elaborate
speeches, this kind of Christian preaching was to be the most
important of all. The development of such preaching also
raises a great many difficult problems only a few of which
can be touched upon here.

(a) In the First Gospel there are some great speeches of
Jesus which are intended to illustrate how He gave instruction
to His disciples. We must not speak of education here, but
of instruction, for the disciples are to be prepared for their
mission in the world as the Lord's messengers. The principal speeches in question are the Sermon on the Mount in
Matthew v–vii, the missionary instruction of the Twelve in
ix. 37–xi. 1, and the disciplinary ordinances in chapter xviii.
No doubt the composition of these speeches was the work of
the Evangelist, for in the other Gospels similar sayings appear
in scattered contexts. It may be historically true, however,
that Jesus preached to His disciples in a similar way, and
that these and corresponding sayings are fragments of His
speeches. Nothing prevents our supposing that Jesus gave
instruction to His disciples in a more continuous form, like
the speeches mentioned.[2] On the contrary, this assumption
will help us to explain why the Apostles instructed the

---

[1] Compare 2 Clem. viii. 1 f.: *hōs oun esmen epi gēs, metanoēsōmen: pēlos gar
esmen* . . . or the first of Luther's 95 theses of 1517: "Dominus et magister
noster Jesus Christus, dicendo 'penitentiam agite', etc. (Matt. iv. 17), omnem
vitam fidelium penitentiam esse voluit."

[2] There are many other views about the teaching of Jesus, but here it is only
a question of His preaching. Otherwise see, for instance, W. A. Curtis, *Jesus
Christ the Teacher* (1943; 3rd impr. 1945), pp. 66–107.

churches in epistles which are in fact written editions of ethical and disciplinary discourses. Moreover, there are pre-Christian analogies to the teaching speeches reported by the First Gospel, especially in the Damascus Fragments.[1] They embody the moral teaching and discipline of the so-called New Covenant of Damascus, but the whole text is presented as a speech delivered by their leader. This is but one of many analogies between these Fragments and the New Testament. It seems to have been normal for a founder of a new community to summarize his instruction in a speech. In this sense the great speeches of the First Gospel may be based upon historical truth.

(b) The apostolic epistles are not sermons; they are just letters. But great parts of them were obviously influenced by oral discourses, such as were commonly delivered by the Apostles, and they may often be regarded as literary substitutes for personal addresses (cp. 2 Cor. x. 10). Phrases such as "brethren", "I say", "you know yourselves" are numerous in the Pauline epistles, and together with the general stylistic character of the epistles and many other facts they prove that the Apostle, when he wrote, imagined himself to be speaking to a collective audience, and not writing to individual readers. The dialogue character of his writing was probably also influenced by the Greek "diatribe".[2] It is also an established fact that the epistles were intended to be read aloud in the churches (Col. iv. 16). So it is legitimate to use the epistles for the study of apostolic preaching.

Large sections of the epistles are concerned with practical questions of discipline and ethics. As Jesus included similar teaching in His discourses, it is natural to conclude that as His disciples, the Apostles imitated the forms of practical instruction which He used. There is evidence to show the authority that Paul as well as his readers attached to the

---

[1] Bo Reicke, *The Jewish "Damascus Documents" and the New Testament* (1946), p. 9 ff.

[2] R. Bultmann, *Der Stil der paulinischen Predigt und die kynisch-stoische Diatribe* (1910); R. O. P. Taylor, *The Groundwork of the Gospels* (1946), pp. 75–90; W. B. Sedgwick, "The Origin of the Sermon", *Hibbert Journ.*, xlv. 2 (1947), pp. 158–164; R. Leijs, "Prédication des Apôtres", *Nouv. rev. théol.*, lxxix. (1947), pp. 610–617.

words of Jesus in disciplinary and ethical problems in the discussion of marriage in 1 Corinthians vii. 8 ff.[1] In addition the Epistle of James may be instanced as an interesting example of ethical and disciplinary instruction. In patristic times, it is remarkable that many Church Orders still have the form of discourses spoken by the Apostles. This seems to follow the early usage whereby the Apostles, as the successors of the Lord, gave oral instruction in matters of discipline. A witness to this usage is the First Epistle of Clement which was sent from Rome to Corinth. It is an epistle and not a sermon, but was obviously written to be read aloud by some person because everyone could not possibly read such a long document; so it was influenced by rhetoric. All these forms can be traced to Jesus, with the Apostles as intermediaries. On the other hand, there are also elements of apostolic preaching which do not seem to have counterparts in the teaching of Jesus, as for instance the *Haustafeln.*

Presumably the apostolic epistles were always intended to be read at meetings of the Church. This sets a ritual character on the exhortations and advice given in these epistles. For it is likely that every Christian meeting had some ritual form (cp. *epi to auto*, Acts i. 15, etc.). Here the question arises whether these exhortations were also expositions of scriptural passages, so that they may be compared with synagogal or later Christian preaching. Perhaps this was sometimes the case. But there is nothing to prove that apostolic instruction or exhortation was generally pegged to the appointed lections. Only later are there hints of a close relation between Scripture reading and preaching in the local churches, a subject to be touched upon below.

Here we must take into account another circumstance which necessarily conferred a liturgical character on all instructional and hortatory preaching as it underlies the epistles as well as later writings: their connection with the

---

[1] This use of the Lord's sayings in pastoral work can be regarded as a chief motive for the collection of His words: T. W. Manson, "The Sayings of Jesus", *The Mission and Message of Jesus* (1938; 2nd impr. 1946), p. 301.

sacraments. After the Lord had departed from the world, the sacraments took the place of His physical presence among the Apostles. While the basis of preaching to outsiders was the Lord's own teaching, the instruction and edification of believers were connected with the sacraments. This does not mean that the sacraments were celebrated at every meeting when instruction and exhortation were given; nevertheless the Eucharist gave a liturgical character to the lections and sermons which preceded it, just as the *missa catechumenorum* was a preparation for the celebration of the Eucharist.

Attention may first be directed to baptism. In the Early Church a special form of sermon was delivered to candidates for baptism. Generally it was the bishop who, as baptizer, instructed and exhorted the neophytes and the congregation. Examples of this are the catechetical sermons of Theodore of Mopsuestia and Cyril of Jerusalem, but there are also descriptions in Justin Martyr and the *Apostolic Constitutions*. It is possible to trace this custom back to New Testament times since some of the epistles were apparently influenced by baptismal addresses, namely Ephesians, Colossians and I Peter. They may be interpreted as adaptations of baptismal exhortations, intended to be read aloud as pastoral letters. Ephesians is scarcely a baptismal sermon, but it was apparently composed with an eye to the newly baptized, the references to baptismal ideas being numerous (*e.g.* i. 13, 18, ii. 1 ff. etc.).[1] Colossians has many parallels with Ephesians (*e.g.* ii. 10–13). I Peter can perhaps be considered even more directly as a baptismal address because it says in iii. 21 : *hymas nyn sōzei baptisma*.[2] In any case it was based upon addresses of this kind. Now it is remarkable that in all these writings dogmatic teaching and doxologies are very important. Both of these are best understood as expansions of kerygmatic teaching appropriate in exhortations to neophytes. Sometimes there are allusions to the kerygma

---

[1] N. A. Dahl, "Dopet i Efesierbrevet", *Svensk teol. kvartalskrift*, xxi. (1945), pp. 85–103.

[2] W. Bornemann, "Der erste Petrusbrief—eine Taufrede des Silvanus?" *Zeitschr. f. d. neutest. Wiss.*, xix. (1919–20), pp. 143–165.

itself, as in 1 Peter iii. 19, 21. In these ways the baptismal sermons are a mixture of what we have called invitation and instruction or edification, the former being represented by the kerygma in an expanded and elaborate form, the latter by the parenesis. Ephesians, which divides into two parts, chapters i–iii and iv–vi, illustrates this double form. As baptism was so central to early Christian thought, apostolic preaching to believers was probably always in some degree related to baptism. The evidence also proves that the Apostles constantly referred to baptism when addressing the members of a Church (Rom. vi. 3 ff.; 1 Cor. vi. 11, etc.). Both in their dogmatic and soteriological teaching and in their parenetic instruction they reminded the believers of what they had learnt; but all their instruction was intimately related to baptism (cp. Heb. vi. 2). In the same way the dogmatic and laudatory sermons that were to be equally important in later preaching, as well as the detailed exhortations that were usual in all preaching, may be understood as elaborations of baptismal instruction. A specimen of elaborate dogmatic and laudatory preaching in the New Testament is the Epistle to the Hebrews.[1] Its rhetorical character is obvious (ii. 5, v. 11, vi. 1, viii. 1, ix. 5, xiii. 22). See especially v. 12–vi. 2, where advanced instruction is explicitly said to be a continuation of the *baptismōn didachē*. This is also Paul's opinion in 1 Corinthians iii. 1 ff. A comparable writing, reflecting dogmatic preaching and yet presented as an apostolic epistle, is the Epistle of Barnabas. The first half is dogmatic; the second half (chapters xviii–xxi) is parenetic (the Two Ways). This division corresponds to that of baptismal sermons as illustrated by Ephesians. Even if Barnabas is a polemical writing it serves to demonstrate the fundamental importance of baptismal preaching for early Christian tradition. (Compare also the direct allusions to baptism in Barnabas i. 2 ff., vi. 8–19 [2] and elsewhere.)

[1] This is the view of J. Berger, "Der Brief an die Hebräer, eine Homilie", *Göttinger Theol. Bibliothek*, iii. 3 (1797), p. 449 ff., and of several later writers.

[2] N. A. Dahl, "La terre où coulent le lait et le miel selon Barnabé 6. 8–19", *Aux sources de la tradition chrétienne*. *Mélanges M. Goguel* (1950), p. 67 ff.

Further liturgical features were conferred upon apostolic preaching by its connection with the Eucharist. It is probable that, if there were any services at all without communion in the early days before special catechumen services had developed, the presence of an Apostle would be the occasion of a communion as in Acts xx. 7, because this was the most intimate form of divine service. Consequently apostolic instruction as reflected in the epistles seems to have had a primary basis in the sacred meal. This assumption is partly confirmed by the striking way in which problems of table-fellowship are touched upon in the epistles (Rom. xiv. 1 ff. etc.).

There is also historical evidence for this opinion. According to Acts ii. 42, the service of the earliest Christian society consisted "in the apostles' teaching and fellowship, in the breaking of bread and the prayers". This connection of teaching and a common meal had a precedent in earlier customs. Jesus gave instruction at common meals (Luke xiv. 1 ff. etc.), and it was a duty of the Jewish paterfamilias to impart religious knowledge at the Passover. The Apostles may have continued such customs. Teaching is not quite the same as preaching, but it is a preparation for it. Continuity is proved by Acts vi. 4, where the prayers of the Apostles are connected with their "ministry of the word" instead of with their teaching as in ii. 42. Further evidence is the description of Paul in Troas (Acts xx. 7 ff.): "And upon the first day of the week, when the disciples came together to break bread, Paul preached (*dielegeto*) unto them . . . and continued his speech until midnight." So the earliest teaching and preaching of the Church were related to the common meal. Even later, when visiting the Christian communities, the Apostles preached to them at the common meal. All this gave a liturgical character to apostolic preaching.

The fact that the Apostles themselves gave instruction to the new community in Jerusalem is of extraordinary interest. It is reasonable to suppose that their instruction concerned not only morals, but also facts about Jesus. What the

Apostles remembered of His life and His sayings was taught to new believers. This seems to have been decisive for the formation of Gospel traditions. In conversion preaching, or the kerygma, the details of the Master's life were not yet of importance. But among believers, and in connection with the Eucharist, these details gained interest. It is thus of great importance that the passion story was the central part of the Gospel tradition.[1]

(c) Leaving the Apostles and turning to ordinary congregational preaching of an instructional and hortatory character, we sometimes find the same forms of preaching as with the Apostles, and sometimes more detailed forms. Evidence of hortatory sermons without any mention of the sacraments is found in 1 Timothy iv. 11–13; 2 Timothy iv. 2 (*eucairōs acairōs*, thus not only in a liturgical context), and Ign. *Ad Pol.* v. 1, the latter passage containing the sketch of a *Haustafel*. Probably the combination "reading, exhortation, teaching" in 1 Timothy iv. 13 means that preaching was associated in Jewish fashion with Scripture reading as in Just. *Apol. I*, lxvii. This practice may accordingly have begun in apostolic times although there is otherwise no early evidence for it. A passage like 1 Corinthians xiv. 26 which mentions psalms together with teaching is of uncertain value because it describes a shapeless service. In later times there could be much variety of form as is shown by Tert. *De anim.* ix.: "iam vero prout scripturæ leguntur aut psalmi canuntur aut allocutiones proferuntur aut petitiones deleguntur." (The word "psalms" in these passages does not mean set lessons, but enthusiastic songs; cf. Eph. v. 19; Col. iii. 16.)

The relation to baptism is still more clear. We think that the so-called *Second Epistle of Clement* is best understood as a baptismal sermon. It has the special purpose of warning believers to be quiet and satisfied with their social position;

---

[1] Hypotheses concerning liturgical influences on the formation of Gospel traditions have been suggested by several authors. Among recent works are R. O. P. Taylor, *The Groundwork of the Gospels* (1946), p. 54 ff., who quotes P. Levertoff's introduction to Matthew. A comparable thesis is that of M. Dibelius, *Formgeschichte*, p. 12 ff., that preaching was the medium of disseminating popular memories of Jesus. But the importance of Acts ii. 42 seems to have been generally neglected.

but on the whole the speaker addresses neophytes as is evident from many expressions such as the following:—

vi. 9: *tērēsōmen to baptisma hagnon*
viii. 6: *tērēsate tēn sphragida aspilon*
xix. 1: *metanoēsai ex holēs cardias*
xix. 1: *scopon pasi tois neois* (the catechumens) *thēsomen*.

Thus what has been called the earliest congregational sermon of the Church should be regarded more specifically as a baptismal sermon, and as a proof of the great significance of baptism for ethical preaching in post-apostolic times. A remarkable detail is the passage 2 Clement xix. 1 which indicates that reading of the Holy Scripture preceded the sermon. This has an analogy in a later baptismal sermon which is perhaps the next most interesting specimen of early baptismal preaching: the *Logos eis ta hagia Theophaneia*, published among the writings of Hippolytus.[1]

On the other hand, the close relationship of instructional and hortatory sermons to the Eucharist seems to have disappeared soon after apostolic times. In 1 Corinthians xiv. 26 extempore teaching is mentioned among the individual contributions of the brethren when they came together. As in Paul's language about "coming together" implies eating the Lord's Supper (xi. 20), probably the Apostle is also concerned in chapter xiv with questions relating to the Eucharist. If so, we may assume that even the teaching referred to in 1 Corinthians xiv. 26 was directly connected with the Lord's Supper. But later texts do not show so close a relationship. Preaching was obviously separated from the Eucharist when a special first part of the service developed which included preaching on a Biblical text, that is, the *missa catechumenorum*. It seems likely that the evolution of a special service for the uninitiated meant an assimilation to the service of the synagogue. Anyhow, the liturgical sermon was adapted to a new context. It lost

---

[1] First utilized for the history of Christian preaching by R. Rothe and A. Trümpelmann, *Geschichte der Predigt* (1881), p. 484 ff., but later neglected. Its authenticity is contested, but for the present purpose the question of authorship is not important.

its immediate association with the Eucharist and was, for the sake of the catechumens, influenced by conversion motifs.

These appear to be the principal factors regarding early instructional preaching.

In the patristic period there are more factors to be taken into account. Above all there are three homiletic forms which acquired considerable importance. We shall call them "encomium", "homily" and "diatribe", and make a few remarks on each of these forms.

The panegyric on Christ and His actions was a rhetorical form highly esteemed by patristic orators, not least by the Syrian fathers. Using a Greek term we shall call it an "encomium". Its occasion was a festival day, and its existence was due to the *de tempore* principle. As the feasts of the Christian year began to develop, a special rhetorical form was evolved to suit them. Because later Christian instances of this form were so much influenced by Greek panegyrics, it might be supposed that the encomium had developed from Greek patterns. This would not, however, be the whole truth. There was already a precedent in the festival days of the Old Testament, for example in Deuteronomy, as well as in many psalms and prophecies. Thus when the Christian encomium appeared it was only a Christian adaptation of earlier panegyric tradition to the celebration of the events of Christ's life. But at the same time it was a "sermon" in the proper sense of the word, as opposed to the exegetical "homily", and stood alongside gentile panegyrics of gods, emperors, kings and magnates. Later these pagan panegyrics had a considerable influence upon the Christian encomiums, especially those of Greek origin. Soon the encomium of Christ was followed by similar eulogies of the martyrs.[1] These seem to be the principal factors in studying the evolution of the Christian encomium. Early patristic evidence for this homiletic form is Melito's *Homily on the Passion*, discovered among the Chester-Beatty papyri [2]; it is a Paschal sermon in the

---

[1] Emphasized by Rothe, *op. cit.*, p. 22.
[2] *Studies and Documents*, xii. (1940), ed. by C. Bonner.

prophetic manner on the Book of Exodus. Hippolytus is said to have delivered a Prosomilia de Laude Domini Salvatoris (Hieron. *De vir. ill.* lxi.) ; it may have been another early specimen of this form which later became so common.

The analytical "homily", or the discursive exegesis of a Biblical text, was also much cultivated by the great preachers of the early Church. In the Alexandrian School Origen was the great master, and it is from his Homilies that we have taken the term, although some earlier Christian writers used it in another sense (for example Ign. *Ad Pol.* v. 1). The immediate prototypes of such discursive homilies were doubtless the Old Testament commentaries of Philo. But the important Hebrew scrolls lately discovered in a cave near the Dead Sea reveal that the practice of circulating such discursive commentaries on Old Testament books was even older, for there is a specimen of this literature in the commentary on Habakkuk.[1] This is the background of "analytical" forms of preaching.

A third form of preaching much cultivated by the patristic orators was the thematic "diatribe" which was originally a rhetorical treatise on a given subject after the manner of the Stoics and Cynics. Its adoption by the Church was the result of the increasing influence of popular Greek rhetoric and philosophy. But there are already traces of it in the New Testament,[2] and in fact it was already used in Hellenistic-Jewish propaganda as is evident from IV Maccabees. Proofs of the great influence of these traditions are to be found in the speeches of the Cappadocian Fathers. This is the background of "thematic" forms of preaching.

(3) *Testament*

(*a*) The farewell speeches of John xiii–xvii have a different character from Our Lord's earlier teaching, because here His intercourse with the Twelve is closer than ever.

---

[1] M. Burrows, J. C. Trever and W. H. Brownlee, *The Dead Sea Scrolls of St Mark's Monastery*, i. (1950), p. xix ff.

[2] See above, note 2, p. 145, where references are given to studies of this subject.

He gives them His testament, and reveals future secrets to them. According to form criticism this is an instance of inherited tradition; the type is to be found in Old Testament traditions concerning a figure who takes leave of his circle and gives them his testament in a form similar to the solemn speech of Jesus on this occasion. (Cp. Gen. xlix, the whole of Deuteronomy, Jos. xxiii–xxiv, Tob. xiv, the *Book of Jubilees* xix. 15–xxii. 30, xxxvi, and, last but not least, the *Testaments of the Twelve Patriarchs*.[1]) Sometimes the account includes a common meal as in the Gospels (*e.g. Test Naphth.* i).[2] Jesus followed these models in His farewell speeches, and the testament in John xiii.–xvii. follows genuine Jewish traditions even if there were also parallels in Hellenism. (Compare further Luke xxii. 21–38 where a shorter discourse is reported, and some passages of the Resurrection narratives.[3]) As was said in the first part of this study, the form which we are discussing may conveniently be called "testament". It is remarkable, however, that our Lord's instruction at the Last Supper corresponds not only to the farewell speeches of the Patriarchs in the passages referred to above, but also to the instruction given by the Jewish paterfamilias at the Passover meal; in fact both are precedents of the Last Supper "testament".

(*b*) The Apostles were also influenced by the testament form. In the first place, Paul's farewell speech in Miletus to the elders of Ephesus (Acts xx. 17–38) is a rhetorical discourse of this kind. Actually it was a farewell for ever (25, 37 f.). Paul commended his own life as a model (18–24, 31*b*, 33–35), urgently exhorted the elders to faithfulness and vigilance in shepherding the flock (28, 31*a*), warned them of dangers to come after his death (29–31), and committed them to the Lord and to the word of his grace (32, as Jesus did to the Paraclete in John xiv. 16, etc.). The same points, with the single exception of the last, are made in 1 Timothy, 2 Timothy and 2 Peter.[4] Reference to the

---

[1] For further details see J. Munck, "Discours d'adieu" (cf. above, note, p. 131), pp. 155–159.
[2] Munck, p. 167, note 2. [3] Munck, p. 165 ff. [4] Munck, pp. 161–163.

Apostle's approaching death as his reason for writing is found in 2 Timothy iv. 6–8 and 2 Peter i. 14; if it is less clear in 1 Timothy there is at least a hint of it in vi. 20, and, for the rest, this epistle is completely based upon testament motifs.[1] From the point of view of form criticism these three epistles and the speech in Acts xx. 17–38 may thus be said to contain obvious, if indirect, specimens of the literary form called testament. Later imitations of the genre are to be found in the *Acta Andreæ*, xv–xviii, and the *Acta Joannis*, cvi–cx (including eucharistic communion). Now these are literary texts and do not prove that such forms of instruction constituted a living, oral tradition in the Early Church. But if the speech of Paul to the elders of Ephesus was faithfully reported there is nothing to exclude the possibility. The epistles mentioned were also influenced by rhetoric, so that it is fair to use their "testament" passages to illustrate forms of Christian preaching.

(*c*) Ordinary ministers presumably did not leave such testaments when departing this life; to do so was a privilege of the Apostles. Only martyrs could possibly follow the same tradition, and they only with considerable variation of form. It is characteristic that Ignatius, as a saint and a martyr, gave exhortations to the congregations of Asia Minor when travelling to Rome for martyrdom, but that he would not imitate the Apostles when composing his addresses (Ign. *Ad Eph.* iii. 1; *Ad Rom.* iv. 3). Besides, there is no trace of revelation or of prophetic pronouncement in the epistles of Ignatius. So these epistles are not formally heirs of the Biblical testaments; only a slight similarity can be alleged. But to judge from the Acts of the Martyrs the form may have survived among the martyrs to a greater extent than can be supported by historical evidence.

(4) *Revelation*

In the Bible, eschatological and metaphysical passages are often different from other kinds of teaching because they

---

[1] Munck, p. 162.

more directly presuppose supernatural experience of another world. This is why such passages, in so far as they have a clear rhetorical form, may be treated as a special kind of preaching. It will here be termed "revelation", in which is included prophetic as well as apocalyptic preaching. As revelation is especially concerned with things to come, it is logically the last of the preaching forms. However, we must insist once again that there are no strict boundaries between the forms. Revelation is necessarily a feature of all the other forms, because of their eschatological bearing. But we must treat revelation independently in its own right because it followed special traditions in Judaism.

With regard to the way in which the bearers of revelation received their message there are two traditional forms: revelations in ecstasy and revelations after death, illustrated respectively by the instances of Ezekiel and Enoch. Not all revelations depended on such antecedent experiences, whether real or pretended. There were also school traditions which drew out the sense of primary revelation by ordinary rational means, and which may therefore be called secondary revelation. Often this coincided with plain instruction, as in many rabbinical instances. It is often difficult to decide whether a revelation is primary or secondary. But by paying attention to these general varieties of revelation an understanding of early Christian revelation can be gained. The handing down of traditions from Jesus to the Apostles cannot rightly be discussed here, for Jesus had a unique position even from a purely formal point of view.

(a) According to the canonical writings Jesus did not practice ecstatic revelation in the technical sense of the word.[1] So far as we know He did not describe experiences gained in a higher world. There are no stories about Jesus comparable with the ecstatic visions of the prophets or the apocalyptists.[2] In fact, this would have been contrary to the whole conception of Him as the Incarnate, the Son. He had all

[1] T. W. Manson, *The Teaching of Jesus* (2nd ed., 1935), p. 260 ff.; J. W. Bowman, *The Intention of Jesus* (1945), p. 53 ff.

[2] Jesus hardly ever spoke explicitly of Himself as a prophet: C. K. Barrett, *The Holy Spirit and the Gospel Tradition* (1947), pp. 94–99.

knowledge from the beginning, and was Himself Wisdom (Matt. xi. 27; Luke ii. 47; John vii. 29; 1 Cor. i. 24, 30; Col. ii. 3). He did not need any ecstatic source of knowledge. Yet, from another point of view, every word that Jesus said was revelation, whether He told His audience the secrets of the Kingdom and the purposes of God, or taught His disciples how to follow Him in faith and love. For He was Himself revelation (Matt. iv. 16, etc.). He spoke with divine authority (Mark i. 22, etc.). His advent and message were throughout related to eschatology.[1] We must recognize that Jesus always communicated revelation although He is not described as a specialist in revelation. This paradox is resolved if we consider that for other men revelation involves their fresh acquisition of a novel and alien kind of knowledge, while in Jesus Christ the subject and the object of revelation were one and the same.

Nevertheless it is legitimate to distinguish certain sayings of Jesus as revelation in a limited sense of the word, because they refer mainly to future events. The Synoptic Evangelists collected these eschatological logia in an apocalyptic discourse (Matt. xxiv. and parallels). Otherwise it is remarkable how slightly revelation of this kind, which was extremely common in contemporary Jewish circles, is represented in our Lord's teaching. There is practically no cosmology or metaphysics, and very little futurist eschatology besides Matthew xxiv. and parallels. Divine secrets were only told in concentrated and concealed forms, in metaphors and parables. The parables especially may be held to represent our Lord's revelational preaching.

The form of preaching which we have called revelation after death is ascribed to Jesus in Matthew xxviii. 18 (only a short phrase, but perhaps meant to be the abstract of a longer speech), 1 Peter iii. 19 (a reference to his preaching to the spirits in prison), and Revelation i. 17 ff. etc. (long statements of the Risen Lord); cf. Melito's *Homily on the*

---

[1] Even if "eschatology" is only a part of the whole historical scheme: O. Cullmann, *Christus und die Zeit* (1946), p. 187; O. Linton, "I vad mån är Jesu etik eskatologiskt betingad?" *Svensk teol. kvartalskr.*, xxv. (1949), p. 3 f., 6 f.

Passion, ci. ff. (similar), and also such writings as the so-called *Epistola apostolorum* and *The Testament of our Lord*, i.   These eschatological traditions may be compared with such Old Testament passages as Psalms, xxii. 23 ff. or Isaiah i. 4–11.[1]

(*b*) The Apostles also laid comparatively little stress upon the gift of revelation, even if their message and their whole ministry was likewise eschatological.[2]   They aimed at reproducing the words of the Lord and the kerygma, but they did not parade any claim to initiation in the hidden secrets of heaven and the future.   Such at least is the picture given by the canonical writings of the New Testament.   Outside the Canon there is an Apocalypse of Peter and similar apocalyptic pseudepigrapha.   In the New Testament, however, there are only such reflections of apostolic preaching of revelations as Acts xi. 4–17 (Peter in Joppa), or xxii. 3–21 and xxvi. 9–20 (Paul's conversion, used as a topic for preaching). Descriptions of divine appearances like these may certainly be treated as revelation.   It can perhaps even be assumed that the Apostles often appealed to similar visions in their preaching, as is the case in 1 Corinthians ix. 1, xv. 3–8; witness to the Risen Christ was also, as was noticed above, a standard item of the kerygma.   But this is not the same as the prophetic and apocalyptic revelations which were so popular in apostolic times.   One can see from Paul's Epistles to the Corinthians that revelation was highly esteemed in Corinth.   Some *hyperlian apostoloi* had success on account of supernatural revelations.   Paul, however, had no wish to glory in celestial visions although he too had received them (1 Cor. ii. 6–16; 2 Cor. xii. 1–5).   This does not mean that Paul rejected the popular use of revelation in preaching, but only that he required it to be controlled and not overestimated (1 Cor. xiv. 26–40).

All these apostolic revelations seem to be of the ecstatic kind. If there were revelations after death connected with the Apostles and their successors, they do not appear in the preaching.

(*c*) The rapid development of revelational preaching in

---

[1] Bo Reicke, *The Disobedient Spirits and Christian Baptism* (1946), p. 234 f.
[2] A. Fridrichsen, *The Apostle and His Message* (1947), p. 4.

the Early Church had its effect among ordinary Christians. When revelation became widely known it was consciously assimilated to Old Testament prophecy and late Jewish apocalyptic. But if sometimes, as in Corinth, it was practised by almost everybody, this was primarily because the Holy Ghost had been given to the whole congregation. The first evidence for such general endowment with the gift of revelation was the Pentecostal miracle. It was expressly interpreted as the pouring out of the Holy Ghost (Acts ii. 17 f.), but also as a fulfilment of the prediction in Joel ii. 28 that all should prophesy. At Corinth as in Jerusalem, enthusiasm was so great that any member of the congregation would stand up in the service and utter prophecies (1 Cor. xii. 8 ff., xiv. 26–40; cf. Rom. xii. 6). In these cases it does not matter whether their preaching was in tongues or not; the gift of revelation was fairly common. But the Early Church also had specialists in revelation who were actually called "prophets" (Acts xi. 27, xiii. 1, xv. 32, xxi. 9–10; 1 Cor. xii. 28 f.; Eph. iv. 11). They seem to have played an important part in early Christian preaching, since they are mentioned so frequently. This congregational preaching is certainly reflected in the abundant apocalyptic literature of the Early Church, although many of the apocalypses are elaborate literary works. This is true of the most important of these writings, the Revelation of St John the Divine. For even if this wonderful revelation is in many ways unique among the Christian apocalypses, it probably illustrates general revelational preaching in the churches of Asia. However, it must be admitted that not all who practised revelational preaching in the Early Church seem to have made such a legitimate use of the Holy Spirit; compare the warnings of Paul in 1 Corinthians xiv. 1 ff. Later specimens of revelational preaching also give an impression of great extravagance. For the rest, the most important fact to be observed in this vast literature is perhaps its generous adoption of Oriental and especially Jewish traditions. Many writings are simply Jewish apocalypses with slight Christian additions, such as the *Ascension of Isaiah* and the

159

Sibylline Books.[1] These works are not sermons, but (we should like to emphasize) they may be studied as reflecting oral sermons.

III. CONCLUSION

This is how the present author would like to group the principal forms and elements of early Christian preaching. He can only give a sketch, and indicate what seem the most important facts and influences. But the survey may prove useful for studies in a field which should, perhaps, be more cultivated in modern theology. It seems worth while to emphasize the following conclusions. (i) In the Early Church preaching was related to the whole corpus of traditions. Attention has to be paid to all the principal forms and their mutual relations. In this context one must not forget the oral basis of the traditions. Further, it is worth noticing that a classification of the types, like that proposed above, is not to be made on purely formal grounds, but to illustrate how the whole corpus of traditions constituted an organic whole. It is thus particularly important to observe the effect of "the apostolic succession", if we may use this expression to describe the transmission of the message as well as its forms from Jesus to the Apostles, and from them to other preachers.[2] (ii) The forms of the apostolic preaching varied considerably in view of the purposes of the preacher. These purposes were discussed here as (1) conversion, including admonition and invitation; (2) instruction and edification; (3) testament; (4) revelation. We saw how the Word was taught in these forms and how they were handed down from (a) Jesus to (b) the Apostles and (c) ordinary preachers.

If this summary provides a starting-point for further study, our purpose will have been well served.

[1] E. Hennecke, *Neutestamentliche Apokryphen* (2nd ed., 1924), pp. 290–472. On apocalyptic in general, see H. H. Rowley, *The Relevance of Apocalyptic* (1944), p. 91 ff.; P. E. Davies, "The Relevance of Apocalyptic for Ancient and Modern Situations"; H. R. Willoughby, *The Study of the Bible To-day and To-morrow* (1947), pp. 279–297; T. W. Manson, "Some Reflections on Apocalyptic", *Aux sources de la tradition chrétienne. Mélanges M. Goguel* (1950), pp. 138–145.

[2] The relation between the apostolic preaching and that of Jesus Christ is also emphasized by Dodd, *The Apostolic Preaching and its Developments*, p. 75.